DATE DUE

~~DE 18 '98~~			
~~MY 14 '99~~			
~~NO 19 '99~~			
~~MY 12 04~~			
~~AP 1 0 06~~			
AP 2 8 08			

DEMCO 38-296

RICHARD SASANOW

T·H·E

401(k)

BOOK

Your Last Best Hope
for Retirement Savings!

· AN OWL BOOK ·

HENRY HOLT AND COMPANY | NEW YORK

Henry Holt and Company, Inc.
Publishers since 1866
115 West 18th Street
New York, New York 10011

Henry Holt® is a registered
trademark of Henry Holt and Company, Inc.

Library of Congress Cataloging-in-Publication Data
Sasanow, Richard.
The 401(k) book : your last best hope for retirement savings! /
Richard Sasanow.—1st ed.
p.   cm.
"An Owl book."
Includes index.
1. Finance, Personal.   2. 401(k) plans.   3. Retirement—
United States—Planning.   I. Title.
HG 179.S239   1996   95-32614
332.024'01—dc20   CIP

ISBN 0-8050-3962-7

Henry Holt books are available for special
promotions and premiums. For details contact:
Director, Special Markets.

First Edition—1996

Designed by Victoria Hartman

Printed in the United States of America
All first editions are printed on acid-free paper. ∞

1   3   5   7   9   10   8   6   4   2

To my mother and father,
who always encouraged me;
to Sydney and Alexa,
who had to live through it all;
and especially to Terri,
for not throwing me out a window.

Contents

Acknowledgments

Thanks to everyone I interviewed about their 401(k)s. You convinced me that this book was worth doing, and it would not have happened without you.

My appreciation goes out to my agent, Faith Hamlin, for thinking that this was "a live one," and to Ed Myers for introducing me to her. Gratitude to my editor, David Sobel, for arm-wrestling me on many points—and actually letting me win a few (I think).

Merci beaucoup to Deborah Batterman and Joan Westreich, for their eagle eyes; Peter Simpson, for his investment knowledge; and especially to Gerry Sachs, copy consultant extraordinaire. To Albert L. Bernstein, CPA, and Susan Yerger, CPA, for their technical assistance; and to the AICPA, which helped me find Isabelle Curtis, CPA-PFP, who was of great help regarding distributions. And to Chris Parker: I'm glad you were around when I'd decided to "abandon ship."

Introduction: Yes, You Have the Power to Take Control of Your Financial Future

It has always been said that only two things in life are certain—death and taxes. Well, I can think of a third: You're going to need more for retirement than you ever dreamed.

How are you going to pay for it? There isn't one simple answer—but your company's 401(k) plan can play an important role in making your future much more comfortable.

> If you're already holding this book in your hand, you probably have an inkling of how powerful a force your 401(k) can be in helping to build up your nest egg.

My goal is to help you get the most out of your 401(k)—and I'm here to blow a bugle, crash some cymbals, beat the drums and let you know that you have the power to use this plan to make your future better, and in some cases, much better.

Taking Charge of Your Destiny

The 401(k) is probably the best way for you take charge of your future, and believe it or not it, you can do it. Approved by the Internal Revenue Code, sponsored by your company, and funded by you (with some help from your employer, if you're lucky), the 401(k) allows you to set aside pretax money for your retirement and reap benefits both now and later.

How does it do this? Think back for a moment to the first time you saved in what you considered "a big way." It was probably a savings plan—a Christmas Club or Vacation Club—from your local bank. You probably put in a buck or two every week, had a little page torn out of your club booklet, and, at the end of a year, got a check for $50 or $100. If you were lucky, you got 2 or 3 percent interest.

Now, your 401(k) is a savings plan, too—think of it as your b-i-i-i-i-i-i-g Vacation Club, which is going to fund the longest vacation you ever have. It's a much better deal that those other clubs, because the money in it can grow and grow in lots of ways:

- You don't pay taxes on the money you contribute until it's time to take it out.
- Deposits come directly from your paycheck—no trip to the bank.
- The funds you contribute may grow substantially—as only investments in the stock market can.
- Compounding could help double your money in seven years (or less)—and then triple it even faster.

Plus:

- Most employers match contributions—usually up to 6 percent of your salary.
- If company stock is part of your plan, you may see it double or triple in value, should you be there when business is great or during a merger or acquisition.

Far, Far Away?

Oh, I know, you think that retirement is too far away, or that someone else will take care of it, or that you can start saving later on in your life. But let me tell you: No matter how old you are—or how young you are—the best time to start saving is now, because *time* is your greatest asset in saving through this kind of plan.

Here's a great example of what setting aside a small amount on a regular basis can do for you:

> If you contribute $100 a month—that's $25 a week—to your 401(k) at age twenty-five, and put it into a stock fund that performs pretty well (say, 9 percent per year) and keep adding this modest amount every month, guess how much you'll have at sixty-five? Nearly half a million dollars! (And if your boss coughs up a 50 percent match for your contribution, the number becomes over $700,000.)

How does this happen, when you've contributed only $48,000? It's not magic—it's the beauty of investing. I'll explain more about it later in the book.

You can start later, of course, and still end up with a nice little nest egg, but it won't be nearly as large: Save $100 a month from age thirty-five, and you'll end up with about $185,000. It goes way downhill from here: from forty-five, $67,000; from fifty-five, $19,500.

Nothing beats starting early. If you start later, you can't catch up even by doubling amounts: Start saving $200 a month at thirty-five instead of $100 at twenty-five and you'll end up with $100,000 less at sixty-five—even though you've contributed $24,000 more!

It's About <u>You</u>

Do you think I've been talking too much about your role in funding your future? Well, welcome to the brave new world of retirement.

It's no longer about what *your* company or *your* government is going to provide for you. If you've read a newspaper or watched the evening news lately, you ought to know that you can't count on anybody to support you in your retirement (unless you have awfully nice, and rich, children).

It's about *you*—and the choices you have to make to make your life better. One of those choices is to join your company's 401(k), but you have to know something very important right from the start: In order to get the most out of it, you have to give up your comfortable position as a *saver*, with your money insured against loss.

> From this minute on, you have to start thinking like an *investor*, because being in a 401(k) isn't just putting aside money for future needs. It's entering the wild world of Wall Street, where there are no guarantees, but lots of opportunities.

In joining the 20 million other American workers in 401(k)s, you're part of a nationwide trend. Not long ago, an article in *Money* magazine proclaimed, "We've shifted from a nation of CD savers to stock fund investors." Well, welcome to the club, but let me ask you one question: *Did anybody ask you if you wanted to join?*

I'll bet the answer is a resounding NO! Chances are good that you might even think of yourself along the same lines as those in a recent survey of 401(k) participants: Fifty-eight percent said that they didn't know how to invest, with 71 percent of the women answering that investing was a foreign language to them.

But that shouldn't keep you from appreciating—and seizing—the opportunity to change your life and *become* an investor, and use this newfound expertise to help fund your future. *The 401(k) Book* can act as your translator and guide to this strange land—and help you to feel at home there.

Stop Acting As If There's No Tomorrow

I've written this book so that you and other 401(k) participants—and those who *can* and *should* be participating—have
step-by-step help that can *empower* you in dealing with it. I
want to help you to get the most out of the only retirement plan
that many people will ever have.

Don't expect this book to tell you which mutual funds to
choose in order to triple your money, because you can stash
your cash only in the investments that are offered by your particular plan. What this book can do is help you get the most out
of the opportunities in front of you—*including the choice of
whether or not to participate.*

I find it shocking that there are still people not participating
in the plans available to them. I'm not talking about clerks making $15,000 who feel they need every cent in their paychecks to
get by each week, and probably do. (Amazingly, though, there
are many workers at this income level who do participate.)

No, I'm referring to the thousands—tens of thousands—of
people who are eligible to use plans, should be participating,
and don't bother to do so. I'm also talking about those who participate at a minimum level or set aside only enough to get the
matching contribution that their companies provide, even
though they can afford to set aside more.

Most of these people don't have any idea that making automatic contributions to the plan won't even affect their pay-
checks very much. (This is particularly true if they lower their
tax withholding for the amount they plan to contribute.) They
don't know that putting aside as much as possible right now can
really make a difference down the road.

> If your company has a 401(k) and you're not yet participat-
> ing—or if your spouse has access to a plan and doesn't bother
> to use it—I'll give you some good reasons for stopping this
> "insanity" and not letting this valuable key to your future slip
> through your fingers!

The Basics

As you read this book, you may notice that certain basic investment concepts are discussed more than once. Why? Because
when the pollsters from the Gallup organization did a survey in
1992 for New York Life (an insurance company that specializes
in 401(k) plans), they found that many plan participants—that's
you and I—were unclear about those basics of investing.

At least two-thirds of the respondents to the survey said they
were not familiar with some of the basics that make 401(k)
plans such an appealing benefit for just about anyone who
works. These concepts include:

- the benefits of tax-deferral (*one way your money grows so
  well*)
- compounding (*another way your money grows so well*)
- inflation's impact (*why your money* has *to grow so well*)
- what age means to investment risk (*why you can afford to
  take more risks when you're twenty-five than at fifty-five*)

Information about these concepts is not all that most people
need. They may have gotten the message that joining the plan is
a good idea, but once they're in, they have to figure out what to
do with their money. This involves:

- asset allocation (*one way to raise your return and lower investment risk*)

and

- choosing among investment options (*another way to raise
  your return and raise or lower investment risk*)

If you are among those who are not familiar with any or all of
these terms, you will be by the time you finish this book.

Yet another survey (this one from John Hancock Financial
Services) shows that half of those who participated in plans

didn't know some of the most basic aspects of investing. Many participants don't know, for example, that money market funds don't invest in stocks and bonds (but in low-risk securities like Treasury bills or CDs) or that it's a good time to buy a bond fund when interest rates are likely to go *down*.

Now Hear This

Here's one thing I will promise to do in this book: to never forget that you're only human.

Do you *want* to hear about what you're going to need for retirement thirty or forty years from now? Probably not. Do you *need* to hear about what awaits many people? Yes, and here it is: You may have only half of what you will need to live on.

There's no doubt about it: Saving enough to provide for your future is difficult.

But don't get aggravated, annoyed, or upset.

Get moving.

Unfortunately, as a plan participant, you start hearing the scary stuff pretty early. If you've already had your enrollment meeting—with all the bells and whistles to get you to join—you may have chilling recollections of it. Someone probably sat down with you or left you with a personal profile to fill out.

Based on a variety of factors, including your lifestyle and salary expectations, the person running the meeting came up with the astronomical amount you'll need when you retire and how much you should start socking away now.

Many people will spend a half hour filling in the blanks of a personal financial profile and decide to save the maximum they need. I say, "Bravo!" If you have it in you to do this, you are to be congratulated because the fact is, *you can't have too much money put aside for retirement.*

But I don't need to spend my time filling out a form to tell me that I'm not saving enough. I know it. *You should know it, too—even if you're twenty-five and see retirement as a lifetime away.* That's why seeing the future in black and white is not a call to action for everybody.

No More Movies?

In fact, many people, seeing their future in black and white through these profiles, only hear a call to . . . pull the covers over their heads and hide. Not only *don't* they take it as a wake-up call, but just the opposite happens. They become de-motivated. They discover that if they save as much as allowed for as long as they can—and if they stop going out on Saturday night—they *still* won't have enough. (Of course, if you're going out *five* times a week, maybe a little rethinking could be in order.)

I recently received a newsletter on retirement planning from a mutual fund company that encouraged people to give up their afternoon coffee break and save the two dollars a day to put toward retirement planning. (The advice comes, of course, from someone who doesn't have to deprive himself of anything.)

How does this kind of "expert opinion" make you feel? Are you likely to follow it? Many people are not. So they give up and say, "Why bother? I might as well enjoy myself now and throw myself off a cliff when I have to."

You won't read that kind of advice here. Yes, I believe that you should work as hard as you can to provide yourself with a nest egg for tomorrow, but I don't believe that depriving yourself today is the way to do it.

I'm not here to tell you to go into suspended animation and never again go to a movie so you can put every cent you can toward your retirement. I'm not a cop and I'm not your mother.

Take Control

What I do say to you is: *Don't let these things get you down. Save what you can.*

Do your best.

Don't let yourself off the hook because you think it's hopeless and doing your best to put money aside won't be good enough. You've got to do what you can—the best you can—even if it's only so you'll never be able to say, "If only I had . . ."

Doing your best also means sitting down and being truthful with yourself about what you can afford to save. You can't empower yourself to take control of your future if you delude yourself into saving 3 percent of your salary when you can only afford to save 1 percent.

I'm also going to talk to all of you who are already participants in a 401(k) and think you have it all figured out. You're looking at it as a way to save for a house or pay for the kids' education and, yes, many people do just that and are thrilled to death to have all that money available to them. I think it's a mistake and a big one, but we'll get to that later.

As a participant in a few 401(k)s myself, I've seen what the people running them do for us and what they *don't* do for us. Even the brochures and newsletters offered by the best plans do not necessarily help you get organized. What I want is to have everything I need to know about managing this type of plan in one place—so if I have a problem, I can look it up and find answers in language I can understand.

I've also worked as a marketing communications consultant for several companies that set up plans for companies like the one you work for, and seen research that has been done on the needs and attitudes of 401(k) participants. I've talked to lots of people who participate in plans and either have trouble or success in running their own accounts.

I've gotten the message that people *want help,* and I've planned this book to give you the kind of help that others have said they want—and need. For example, you'll find good reasons:

- to get started
- to contribute as much as you can
- *not* to be too conservative in your investment choices
- *not* to borrow against your plan money
- *not* to spend your savings when you change jobs
- to stay with your plan "as long as you both shall live."

HOW TO USE THIS BOOK

• • • • • • • • • • •

"Start at the beginning, and continue through to the end" is the advice that the White Rabbit gave to Alice during her adventures in Wonderland, and I pretty much agree with that guidance for reading this book. (I do caution you, however, not to read too much of it in a single sitting. After all, I don't want anybody to crash and burn from information overload.)

The book's organized so that you can quickly find the specific information you need. Part I, comprising three chapters, outlines all the basic principles of the 401(k) plan, and explains clearly why the plan is so important to your future security. This part tells you how the plans are structured and how they make your money grow so dramatically, and it does away with all excuses you may have used to avoid joining your plan.

Part II is specially designed to be a "crash course" for those of you who are under some kind of time pressure in making your 401(k) decisions. The single chapter in this part will be of particular benefit to readers who, for example, are required to attend a company enrollment meeting before they have time to read the entire book. I've tried to give you a comprehensive overview in this section, touching briefly on all the major aspects of getting started in your 401(k), but remember that all the topics covered in this chapter are explained in much greater depth elsewhere in the book.

Part III provides detailed advice on getting the maximum benefit from your 401(k). We'll discuss the basics of investing, including risk, asset allocation, selecting funds, and understanding the ups and downs of the markets. The last section deals with all the other important aspects of managing your plan, such as job changes, retirement, and withdrawals.

Remember, do the quizzes if you have the patience, if only to introduce the information that follows. (If you don't, that's okay, too.) But at least take the time to look at the answers before moving on, so you don't miss anything that might help your 401(k) grow as large as possible.

After all, no one has earned the right to a comfortable retirement more than you.

PART I

The 401 (k): Why You Need It, What It Is, and What It Can Do for You

1

Why You Need This Book *Now*

In this chapter, I'll discuss why you need to bother having a 401(k) at all. There are big issues involved—bigger than you or I—but, like it or not, they affect all of us and we have to deal with them.

But before we get into it, I have a few questions for you:

DO YOU KNOW . . . ?

1. What's a baby boomer and what will go "boom" around the year 2013?

2. Which can you count on?

    (a) your pension in twenty years

    (b) Social Security

    (c) the color of your socks

3. What's a "three-legged stool" and what happened to it?

4. Cola may not be good for your teeth, but when is a COLA definitely good for your future?

5. How much of your final salary will you probably need, at least, for your retirement?

    (a) 70%

    (b) 95%

    (c) 33⅓%

ANSWERS:

1. The first baby boomers, born between 1946 and 1964, will cause a big boom in the economy when they start retiring around 2013.

2. (c) your socks. Everything else is up for grabs—and possible change.

3. A "three-legged stool" is the traditional description of how to pay for retirement—and it's getting more and more out of date.

4. A COLA, or cost-of-living adjustment, helps pensions and Social Security keep up with inflation.

5. (a) but the more the merrier your retirement can be.

A 401(k) can do some pretty important things for you. It can help you:

- save money as painlessly as possible
- get extra company benefits that are available only to those who participate in a plan
- defer taxes on the money you save, so it grows faster.

Before we get to the good news and how you're going to do things you may never have dreamed of—like investing, maybe investing aggressively—there are a few facts and figures you should know regarding why you have to think about this at all.

More than one in three Americans is a baby boomer, born in the era that started after the troops came home from World War II and ended in 1964.

In 2013, the first baby boomers will retire, their ranks growing by the millions until 2031. They will spend an average of 25 percent of their lives in retirement, or fifteen to twenty years.

Even if you're not a boomer yourself, the sheer numbers who will be entering retirement about the same time will have an impact on your retirement—whether it's the government telling you that you have to start later and expect lower payments, or the numbers competing with you for part-time jobs.

The Way It Should Be:
The "Three-Legged Stool" of Retirement Income

The big question: Where is the money for retirement going to come from? It's a good question.

Years ago, Americans didn't think about retirement. They didn't have to, because someone or other did it for them. It was all part of the old "retirement-as-a-three-legged-stool" analogy.

Leg #1: If you worked for a large company,
you could count on their taking care of you,
in return for thirty years of loyalty.

A generation ago, most people relied on some kind of company pension to help fund their retirement. While the first private pension wasn't created until 1875 by American Express, pensions were as all-American by the mid-1950s as *I Love Lucy*.

Today, all you can count on is . . . not much. There are many reasons that you might not have earned yourself a pension; having chosen to change jobs frequently is only one of them.

> Mergers, cutbacks, reengineering, and bankruptcies are all realities of work life in the nineties, and they all mean one thing: You could find yourself out looking for another job, no matter how loyal you've been.

And even if you are not out, your company's pension plan could leave you out. How can they do this? Easy.

• Some companies decide they can no longer afford this kind of benefit and terminate their plans, so they don't have to contribute any more than they already have. (From '89 to '91 alone, 42,000 employers terminated their retirement plans.)

• Even those plans still around may be *underfunded,* not having enough funds to provide benefits for everyone who is supposed to get them. (Currently, there's $53 billion in shortfalls, not counting the problems of some federal government plans.) The Pension Benefit Guaranty Corporation (PBGC) continues to chase after underfunded plans to get them to put their accounts in order—General Motors, for instance, had to come up with $4 billion for one plan in May 1994—but the PBGC can do only so much.

 • If you work for a small company, you're probably out of luck, because most have always found pensions beyond their means.

So even if you are entitled to a pension, the one you get may be smaller than it should have been, and won't be enough to cover all your expenses by tomorrow's living standards.

Leg #2: If you worked for a smaller business, you could always count on the Social Security system.

When the Social Security Act was passed in 1935, the retirement age was chosen as sixty-five. Why? Because (typical of gifts that the government gives to us) they didn't expect us to be around to collect, since the average life expectancy was pegged at sixty-three. Who got to hold on to all the money that wasn't used? Guess.

While most government officials would swear that Social Security was never meant to be anyone's major source of retirement income, lots of people used to get by on it, for better or worse.

Despite cost-of-living adjustments (COLA) through the years, relying on Social Security for the bulk of your retirement income would be nearly impossible in the current environment. Still, lots of people are counting on Social Security for as much as 50 percent of their retirement income. (And the government keeps threatening to take the COLA away.)

Much more serious today is the question of Social Security's future: Will it still be around for the millions of baby boomers who look forward to putting their feet up and relaxing around 2013 or so? When it was created in 1935, fifty-five workers supported every retiree; today, it's less than three to one, and still falling.

Today, Social Security has a huge surplus from which to pay out benefits, but the federal government keeps borrowing from it for other purposes, depleting its funds. The consensus from the experts is that it will still be around in the next century, but giving less to retirees and starting later than it has in the past; other estimates show that it will be bankrupt by 2030. In addition, income testing may become standard in the future, possibly to exclude higher-paid individuals from getting anything at all.

If all this wasn't bad enough, the government insists on calling Social Security—which we as taxpayers have paid for ourselves!—an "entitlement" payout, which they want to cut in order to shrink the budget deficit.

Leg #3: No matter how generous the other sources of your retirement income, personal savings has always been considered an integral component.

Here's where we come in. The third leg has always been thought to be the few bucks we put away on our own. Let me not underestimate the word *few,* since it's no secret that the savings rate in this country is pathetic—lower than in any other industrialized country in the world.

When Merrill Lynch, a provider of 401(k) plans, surveyed the retirement savings habits of Americans, they found that the average fifty-year-old had the whopping sum of $2,300 in financial assets and savings. Not much to live on.

For many, the few dollars stashed away are in old IRA accounts—you remember, those $2,000 ($2,250 with a stay-at-home spouse) accounts that the government authorized to help us save, with taxes deferred,* for retirement. Then Congress did away with the deduction for most of us, although it may make a comeback one of these days. While these accounts continue to grow (if you didn't withdraw them prematurely when your first bank certificate of deposit was up), many people haven't contributed for years.

On the other hand, things may not be so grim. Research, including a study from management consultants McKinsey & Co., has predicted that the savings rate will increase dramatically in the next twenty years, as baby boomers approach their "golden years" and shift their spending patterns from buying homes and educating children to recognizing the need to save for retirement.

So what do we have to look forward to?

The Way Retirement Could Be

According to the experts, you'll need at least 70 percent or more of your final salary to make a go of it in retirement.

- The Social Security Administration figures that if you are a single person making $57,600 at retirement, Social Security will replace only about 23 percent. (If you have a spouse, it will be at least one-third more. If you're making only $20,000 a year, Social Security will replace nearly a half, although still not enough to live on in real dollars.)
- If you have a company pension, you can expect another 20 percent.
- If you're in shape to work, you can replace another 27 percent. (Of course, there are limits to how much you can make before earnings start cutting into your Social Security benefits, until age seventy.)

---

*IRAs that are still tax-deferred but funded with money that has already been taxed continue to be available to anyone.

How're we doing? That's the 70 percent of your income just before retirement, or just over $40,000. You'll get a little more if you're married. Not much to take you on the grand tour of the world's hot spots. This is particularly true if you have other financial obligations besides your retirement—for example, mortgage, elderly parents, not to mention the education of your children. Estimates are that most people won't even have that.

An article in *Barron's*, a weekly financial newspaper, stated that a married couple, forty-five years old today, with a joint income of $100,000 will end up with only 60 percent of what they'll need in retirement. And that's assuming they're already saving 5 percent to 7 percent of their income. Estimates in a study by the consulting firm Arthur D. Little and the WEFA Group for OppenheimerFunds are even lower. (According to *Business Week*, personal savings as a percentage of the country's wealth—the gross domestic product—dropped from about 6.25 percent to 3.5 percent between 1981 and 1991.)

No wonder 91 percent of those surveyed by the National Taxpayers Union said that retirement is their number-one concern for the future!

"Who—Me Retire?"

Many people don't find the very idea of retirement all that appealing.

There is a growing (but still relatively small) body of opinion that says retirement is bunk—because times have changed. Some people may be ready for all play and no work at sixty-five or sixty-seven, but not everyone is. I don't think I'll be.

The Census Bureau says that by 2040, the average life expectancy will have increased from the current seventy-five to eighty-one. (In fact, some research has shown that the number of Americans reaching the age of one hundred is doubling every ten years—adding up to 500,000 by 2040!)

Worth magazine, a personal finance magazine and subsidiary of Fidelity Investments, reported recently that 25 percent of today's retirees say that they're very unhappy about not being at work. The magazine suggests a kind of "conspiracy" to make people think that they *must* retire at sixty-five or so, when, in fact, there's not really any reason to do so.

While I'm not sure there's any conspiracy, I do know from my own family and acquaintances that not everyone's ready to retire at seventy, or even at eighty or older. There are still plenty of people who want to be carried out, feet first, from their desks, no matter how full the rest of their lives is. To many, "golden years" does not mean sitting in the sun in Albuquerque, but the glow of working because they *want* to.

So, if you like what you do or have no idea of what you're going to do with yourself when you have all that time on your hands, maybe you should reevaluate your options. This might be the perfect opportunity to set aside thoughts of retirement for a moment and think about what you'd like to do for the rest of your life. Retirement planning still has to be part of your strategy for the future, though, even if it's to subsidize the start of a second career.

But if you are planning to retire—you've earned it, you deserve it, and by golly, you're going to do it—saving through a 401(k) can help relieve some concerns that you have (or should have) about retirement income. While I don't pretend that every company's version of the plan is wonderful, it can be a great way to fund your future.

What You Should Have Learned from This Chapter

1. The retirement of 31 million baby boomers early in the next century will change everything—including Social Security benefits.
2. Company-paid pensions are far from extinct, but are increasingly rare—and unlikely to cover all your retirement expenses.
3. Personal savings have always been included as one "leg" of retirement income—but Americans have the worst savings rate in the world.

4. Surveys have shown that most retirees will have only 60 percent—or less—of the money they'll need in retirement.
5. Everyone is not happy in retirement at sixty-five—so think about the alternatives and put it off if you wish to and can.

2

The 401(k): What It Is, How It Works—and Why It's Possibly Your Last Best Hope

Forget Fido. In this chapter, I'll help you understand why the 401(k) is really man's (and woman's) best friend. I'll introduce you to the way it works and why it's going to play a big part in your future.

Before getting started, however, here are some questions:

DO YOU KNOW . . . ?

1. If the "three-legged stool" of retirement income will be there for you?

2. Whether you should complain when you're offered a "salary reduction plan"?

3. Whether your 401(k) is a total loss when you change jobs?

4. Whether your plan gives you "something for nothing"?

5. What Einstein considered "the most powerful force in the universe"?

ANSWERS:

1. No. With private pensions less and less common, and Social Security's future uncertain, the only "leg" you may be able to count on is your own 401(k).

2. A "salary reduction plan" is a bad name for a good deal: the 401(k).

3. No, because it belongs to you.

4. Of course, you've earned it, but if your company matches part of your 401(k) contributions, it may feel like "something for nothing."

5. Compound interest, which can help your money double or triple faster than you can imagine.

You've begun to get the message that it's up to you to make sure that your retirement works. But how do you do it?

Right now, you may already be saving for a house or a vacation or college for the kids. How the heck is retirement—thirty years or more down the road—going to fit into your financial future?

While it is a little hard to envision the federal government as a white knight to the rescue, it has provided us working people with the 401(k) as a different way to save for retirement needs. Uncle Sam wants *you* to set aside part of your salary before it is taxed, invest it, and not pay taxes on any of it (including the growth of your investment) until it's time to retire. Your company has to cooperate, of course, in setting up the plan, but most are only too happy to provide a benefit that is low-cost to them and extremely useful to employees. Indeed, for many of us with no private pension, and with Social Security in question, 401(k) savings will be not so much the center of a three-legged stool as the driving force of our future.

> Chances are good that just about any company you work for during the rest of your life will have a 401(k).

Ninety-eight percent of companies with more than five thousand employees have them; 78 percent of companies with between one thousand and five thousand employees have them. Every other company down to those with fifty employees has been targeted by providers, which include mutual fund companies, insurance companies, and banks.

According to current IRS regulations, contributions to your account, including any company matching and/or profit sharing, cannot exceed 25 percent of your salary or $30,000. Each company sets its own percentage for employee contributions, usually 10 to 15 percent of your salary. Unfortunately, this may not get you to the maximum personal contribution allowed by law, which was $9,240 in 1995.

There's an annual cost-of-living increase built in to help you keep up with inflation—except for 1995. (Did you know that? Congress deleted it to help pay for the international trade agreement, GATT, it approved in December 1994.) Contributions for 1996 should be about $9,500.

Who Knew What It Meant?

When the 401(k) was first introduced, there should have been dancing in the streets. Unfortunately, even those who were offered this excellent benefit didn't know what to make of it.

Why?

> The good news about this new kind of retirement savings plan was hidden behind official terminology: It was designated a "defined contribution plan," whatever the heck that is. But that wasn't the worst of it: There were its two awful names: "401(k)" and "salary reduction plan."

"401(k)" refers to the section of the Internal Revenue Code that gives its blessing to this kind of retirement-planning tool. The plan itself, however, was actually conceived and designed in 1981 by Ted Benna, a benefits consultant, who looked at the regulation and came up with an idea that was not intended by the government, but was accepted by the IRS nonetheless.

As for "salary reduction plan" ... Doesn't this sound like something that you could live without? It may (partially) describe what it does—reduces your current taxable salary by the amount contributed to your company's plan—but who would ever want to join something that lowers our salaries even more than IRS has already done!

No wonder people weren't banging down the door to join.

The Most Beautiful Words: Tax-Deferred Saving

Today, 401(k) plans have become so common that employees are much less likely to turn the page in the benefits booklet when they see it. And yet . . . For some reason, even today, the 401(k)'s benefits remain a mystery to many—and that's a major reason they don't join. According to one study, by KPMG Peat Marwick, only 61 percent of those eligible participate.

> Sure, the 401(k) doesn't measure up to the joys of a company-paid pension. Sure, you mainly pay for it yourself and have the large part of the responsibility for how well it grows. But it still has certain advantages that cannot be overlooked. And participating in it can be the most important step you ever take.

It's very simple to understand, really. Here's a short overview of what happens when you decide to join your company plan:

1. *You give your company permission to automatically set aside a certain percentage of every paycheck, before it is taxed, usually up to $9,240 each year (depending on your salary and the percentage you choose to defer). It's put into an account in your name and your contribution belongs to you and no one else.* *

2. *Usually, your company matches part of your contributions. (More than 80 percent of companies do.) This money will belong to you—depending on a schedule called "vesting" set by the company, usually less than five years. It is* not *included in that $9,240 figure.*

3. *You get to invest it in a variety of ways, which may include*

---

*Some companies also offer supplementary plans allowing contributions on an after-tax basis that also grow tax-deferred.

several stock or bond fund options,* a type of savings account, and company stock.

4. *You can usually adjust the investments you've chosen† at least quarterly and sometimes daily. (Some plans allow only annual changes.) You get a statement of your account's value several times a year, showing any changes you've made in your investment choices and the increase/decrease in its value.*

5. *If you change jobs, you can take your plan money with you; if you stay with your company, most plans allow you to borrow from your account.*

6. *Your account may increase/decrease in value, depending on the stock and bond markets, but you pay no taxes on the amount you contribute to it—or the amount it grows by interest or other kinds of distributions you receive from your mutual funds—until you start to make withdrawals from it when you retire.*

> Tax-deferred investing is perhaps the 401(k)'s most important feature. It's a great bonus for people who haven't been able to save—because their money can grow more quickly.

Instead of paying taxes on your total income, you can postpone payment on the part that you've set aside in your 401(k) and allow it to keep growing until you retire. Adding this amount to your kitty gives you the possibility of doubling or tripling your money faster than you could if your savings were being taxed as you went along.

---

*Your plan may offer mutual funds; alternatively, it may offer vehicles with similar risks and rewards, and I will treat them as interchangeable. These others may include "sub-accounts," provided by an insurance company, or special funds that are created for your organization by its money manager. Some of these other choices may not be listed in newspapers for you to follow or offer detailed descriptions of investment policies.

†There are still some employer-directed plans where employees' money is pooled and managed in a single portfolio.

The True Story of Saving $1,200 Through Your 401(k) Plan Versus Doing It on Your Own

The 401(k) way. Each month, the $100 you have decided to contribute to the plan for the month is deducted before computing the tax on your paycheck, dividing it among your paychecks for the month. It places the money in your 401(k) account, in the investments that you have chosen. If your company is like most, it will match 50 percent of your contribution (up to a maximum it sets), adding, for example, $50 to your account. The account's earnings add to its value until sometime down the road when you make withdrawals (ideally for retirement living).

At the end of a year, it would look something like this, assuming you earned 10 percent on it:

You've contributed	$1,200
Your company has added	$600
A total of	$1,800
You've earned a 10 percent return	$180
Less current taxes	$0
You now have	$1,980
(If your company didn't contribute	$1,320)

Saving $1,200 on your own. In order to save $100 a month on your own, you have to start out with about $139 a month ($1,668 annually) *before* taxes to get there. No one matches your contribution if you save on your own. In fact, the only one who is interested in your savings is the tax collector, so you can pay on your account's earnings. So after all the tax has been taken out of that $1,668, you end up with $1,243.20 (or less, if you pay local taxes where you live).

You've started out with	$1,668
Federal tax gets you down to about	$1,200
Your company has added nothing	$0

A total of	$1,200
You've invested so it's grown 10 percent	$120
You now have	$1,320
Less federal tax (on your growth, 28%)	$33.60
You now have	$1,286.40

Even if you had no company matching in your 401(k), your balance at the start of the next year would be $1,320 versus $1,286—which may not seem like much of a difference, but it took you $468 *more* to get to that *lower* number! What's more, because of compounding, any extra money in your account will grow even faster. (More about this later.)

(Note: You might also hear that saving through your 401(k) has another benefit—to postpone paying taxes on part of your current income until you retire, when you'll probably be in a lower tax bracket. That may not necessarily be true and I wouldn't count on it.)

Painless saving. A 401(k) makes saving about as painless as it's ever going to be. Why? Because your company takes your contribution out of your check before you ever see it . . . and what you don't touch, you can't spend. Some plans call the concept of automatic saving "pay yourself first," which is cute but accurate. It means that *before* you pay the butcher, the baker, and the candlestick maker—and I know there are plenty of others—your 401(k) contribution is deducted from your check and put directly into your plan account. Not only does this simplify your life, but as I've said before, it *actually costs you less* than it seems, because as a pretax contribution, it's worth more.

And for all of you who say, "I don't need this kind of account—I can save by myself," let me remind you of a thing or two. Even if you have the discipline to save on your own, you'll find that taxes reduce the amount you have to save. (See page 19 for more on this.)

Other Plan Benefits You Can Count On

There are other indisputable benefits to saving your hard-earned cash this way, in addition to the tax-deferral aspect:

- It finds money you didn't know you had.
- It can grow impressively.
- It's flexible.
- It's yours.
- It's portable.
- It can be a lifesaver.
- It's hard to get to.

(The last point may not immediately strike you as a benefit, but you'll soon learn why it is.)

Benefit #1: It can help you save money you never thought you had—and does it automatically.

One of the best features of the plan is that your contributions are taken automatically from your paycheck. You don't get the chance to "should-I-or-shouldn't-I." You can't say, "Maybe next month." You won't be able to say, "I can't afford it." The fact is you *can* afford it.

As shown above, your contribution is made with pretax money, which means no federal, state, or local tax (only Social Security/Medicare) is deducted before it goes in. Or think of it the opposite way: If you don't put the money in your 401(k), federal, state, or local tax *will* be taken out of it.

That $100 (for example) you keep won't give you an extra $100 in spending money, anyway: Uncle Sam is waiting to take his cut. (If you live in New York City, as I do, Uncle George [that is, the state] and Uncle Rudolph [the city] take their cuts, too.) You'll also have to pay taxes every year on the income and/or capital gains you earn on the money. With a mutual fund, you may also have to pay a yearly fee or worry about minimum balances.

If you decide to take $100 as income instead of putting it in your plan, you could end up with $70, $60, $50, or less, depending on your salary and where you live.

Once you look at everyone who wants a piece of your paycheck, you'll realize that it's hardly worth it *not* to put that $100 into the plan.

Regular automatic investing has another plus: dollar cost averaging. When you invest in a mutual fund, you are actually purchasing shares in the fund, which vary in price in the same way individual stocks do. As your plan contribution is invested every month or two weeks (depending on how often you receive a paycheck), you buy your shares of the funds at the current price. Therefore you get more shares when the price is low and fewer when the price is high.

For example, if you contribute $100 a month for six months when the price varies, you will get

4	shares when the fund is at	25
5	shares when the fund is at	20
4.44	shares when the fund is at	22.50
4.35	shares when the fund is at	23
5.71	shares when the fund is at	17.50
4.76	shares when the fund is at	21

You end up with

28.26	shares bought at an average price of	21.50

It's one of the ways to take the sting out of the ups and downs of the stock market—because you end up with an average price. (However, if you happen to be in a fund that is taking a fall and is unlikely to recover, averaging doesn't do you much good. That's one of the reasons you have to keep an eye on your investments, as we'll talk about later.)

*Benefit #2: It can grow impressively
because of compounding.*

You'll be amazed how large your savings can grow—particularly if you start early and keep going—through the wonders of *compounding*. Compounding is what happens when your account keeps growing every year not just on your original investment, but also on its growth in previous years. Here's an example:

Say you invested $1,000 in a mutual fund that paid an average of 10 percent for the year, starting on January 1; by the end of the year, it grew by $100. If you make no additional contribution to the account, at the end of the second year, you have $1,100 plus $110, or $1,210. If the same thing happens in the third year, you will have $1,210 plus $121, or $1,331. If the same thing happens in the fourth year, you will have $1,331 plus $133.10, or $1,464.10, and so on.

If you had set aside this money in an account that pays 10 percent simple interest, where the increases are based only on your initial investment, you would have $1,100 at the end of the first year, $1,200 at the end of the second, $1,300 at the end of the third, $1,400 at the end of the fourth, and so on.

The great scientist Albert Einstein called compound interest "the most powerful force in the universe." Believe me, that's no exaggeration. Look at what compounding can do over longer periods for larger sums:

• Keep that $1,000 in that mutual fund just mentioned for ten years and you'll end up with $2,593, which, compared to anything you'd get in a bank, is very good indeed.
• Leave it in for another ten years at the same rate and it becomes $6,727—or more than two and a half times what you had after the first ten years.
• Leave it in for thirty years at that rate and—wow!—it turns into $17,449, or seven times the ten-year rate for only three times the length of time.

> Through the beauty of compounding, your mutual fund shares grow not only in *value*, but also in *number*.

For instance, look at one share of a mutual fund in your plan. It represents pieces of stocks or bonds of lots of companies. The share's price will go up or down, depending on three factors, the first, major one being whether the prices of securities it owns go up or down. The second reason is that it could sell any of its securities, for a price either higher or lower than the one it paid; these are called *gains/losses*. Third, the companies it has invested in could pay a dividend (for stocks) or interest (for bonds). Once deductions are made for any fund expenses and losses, shareholders (you and I) get some of what's left. These are called *distributions*.

> As an individual investor, you have the choice of taking distributions in cash or having them reinvested as additional fractions of a share added to your account. In your 401(k), you don't have a choice; it becomes part of your account.

These gains and distributions become part of your account as additional fractions of a share. So your shares can grow in value and number—and *those* new shares can grow in value and number, and *those* new shares grow in value and number. . . .

Of course, there is also a downside to this: If you have losses in your account, compounding works against you. Say you have saved $1,000 and make 10 percent on it the first year; you end up with $1,100. But the second year, you lose 10 percent. You don't end up in the same place you started, but $1,100 minus $110, or $990, and your investment has to work harder to get back up to where it was the year before. (While I wouldn't spend too much time worrying about this, it *is* a reminder of the risks that you run into when you invest.)

*Benefit #3: It's flexible in the ways
you can invest your money.*

You get options. The vast majority of 401(k)s have several in-vestment options from which you can choose, although a few have a single one. These usually include, at a minimum, a stock fund, a bond fund, some kind of low-risk savings account, and possibly company stock. Buck Consultants, a benefits consult-ing firm, conducted a survey of 465 companies that offer 401(k)s and found that 22 percent had five or more investment options and 94 percent had three or more. Fewer than 2 percent had ten or more options, although other surveys predict this number will be common in half of all plans within the next few years.

You get to divide your contributions among the choices ("op-tions") offered by your plan in any percentage you want (usu-ally in increments of 5 percent to 10 percent). If you want to put all your money in the stock fund, because you want to live ad-venturously in order to possibly get a better return, no one can tell you not to. If you want to leave it in the savings account be-cause you're really scared to death of losing it, you can do that, too, though it's not a good idea.

You get help. Plans generally give you some help in making your choices, although probably not as much as you would like. You'll get a booklet with pie charts or an in-person presentation or the loan of a video that shows you various ways to break up your account (what's known as "asset allocation") at different stages of your life. A few, very generous employers might even offer you access to personal financial planners on your com-pany's premises, but they won't come right out and say which funds you should choose.

About as close as they will get to making specific recommen-dations will be to attempt to make your choices even easier by offering "asset allocation funds" or "lifestyle funds." These funds divide up your contributions among stocks and bonds in different proportions, and change proportions according to various formulas: the performance of the stock and bond markets; your age or number of years to retirement, etc. (See Chapter 8 for more on these funds.)

While you are usually the only one responsible for *choosing* the funds in your portfolio, *managing* your investments is another story.

> Your funds are run by professional portfolio managers and research teams who specifically look for the best investments that meet the fund's objectives.

These watchdogs may do everything from reading financial statements to visiting the company's factory floor to assess a company's worth before buying into it—more digging than most of us could ever hope to do. While you can't get as rich from investing in a mutual fund as you could from a single stock whose value goes through the ceiling, you also have much less of a chance to end up losing your shirt.

You get to change your mind. Many (but not all) plans also let you easily change your mind about which investments you have chosen. Plans with *daily valuation* usually have a toll-free phone line that lets you automatically change your funds and allocations for past or future contributions (or both), at any time of the day or night. Other plans may restrict your account changes to one to four times a year.

Even the most flexible plans usually have restrictions on how often you can make changes, but that's okay. You'll find that trying to outguess the direction of the stock market doesn't really work—especially since your changes aren't carried out until *after* the markets close for the day. I know. I've tried every trick myself, and none of them work.

Benefit #4: It belongs to you alone.

The money in your 401(k) is yours: It has your name written on it. No one can take it away from you. The money you contribute (along with all it earns) belongs to you immediately. The money or stock that your company may have added in matching eventually belongs to you, according to a formula called vesting that you will find in your plan documents. Sometimes you are immediately vested in the company's contributions to your account, but, usually, all of it is yours by the end of five years. Until then, you are entitled to increasing percentages over time.

Benefit #5: It's your faithful companion.

This last point is an important 401(k) benefit that people like me have found very appealing.

You don't have to worry about whether you can get it if you change jobs or lose your job: You can take it with you. I can't tell you how many people never work long enough in one place to ever be eligible for any company's pension plan, but I know that I'm one of them.

Benefit #6: It can be a lifesaver.

Not to be overly dramatic or anything like that, but even if Social Security is still around, it will simply not be enough to let you retire very comfortably. With the help of your 401(k), your life can be closer to the way you would like it to be.

> If you don't do something to fill out the funds you'll need for retirement, you're going to have to cut back your lifestyle at a time when you deserve all the luxuries you can get.

Benefit #7: It's not that easy to reach.

This last point is critical to your success in growing a large account. While the money is yours, it's hard enough to get to so that you don't use it frivolously.

Many plans allow you to borrow from your account without giving a reason, although you still have to pay it back regularly and pay interest to yourself. In the worst-case scenario, if you have a real financial emergency, you may be able to make a hardship withdrawal, but not without showing true need and no other way to handle your problem.

> If you change jobs while a loan from your 401(k) account is outstanding, you have to settle up immediately with your fund administrator or most loans become taxable distributions— and then you have to settle up with Internal Revenue.

However, if you have decided to leave your company, you can take your 401(k) with you in a variety of ways, with no ifs, ands, or buts. You could even decide to leave it where it is until retirement. (See Chapter 9.)

What You Should Have Learned from This Chapter

1. Chances are excellent that any company that you work for during the rest of your life will have a 401(k).
2. Your ability to put away money that has not been taxed is perhaps the greatest feature of the 401(k).
3. Compounding allows your investments to grow faster—to double in seven years, if your fund's return is 10 percent.
4. Automatic deductions help you save in the most painless way—with money you didn't even know was there.
5. The money in your plan is portable, which means that you can take it with you when you change jobs. It always belongs to you.

3

"I Can't Afford to Save" and Nine Other Terrible Excuses for Passing Up Your 401(k)—and the Benefits You'll Miss If You Do

In this chapter, you'll find out that there are no new excuses under the sun for not joining your plan. You'll also have a better understanding of what you're missing if you're saving in some other way—or not saving at all.

Here's a quiz to show you what's ahead:

DO YOU KNOW . . . ?

. . . which of the following statements are true?

1. If you have other expenses, you can't afford to save for retirement.

TRUE _____   FALSE _____

2. If you've never invested before, you can still learn to take care of a 401(k).

TRUE _____   FALSE _____

3. If your company has its own pension plan, you don't have to worry about saving for retirement.

TRUE _____   FALSE _____

4. If your spouse saves at work, you should still start your own 401(k).

TRUE _____   FALSE _____

5. If you're entitled to Social Security, most of your retirement income is set.

TRUE _____   FALSE _____

ANSWERS:

1. False. Saving through a 401(k) gives you access to money that you didn't even know you had.

2. True. Learning to handle your investment dollars is easier than you think.

3. False. Your company's retirement plan isn't designed to satisfy all your needs, even with Social Security thrown in. There's a good chance that it does not have an annual cost-of-living adjustment, which means it will shrink every year.

4. True. As I said before, you can't have enough money if you want a comfortable retirement.

5. False. Even in the best of circumstances, Social Security can be counted on for only a small part of your retirement income needs.

When it comes to deciding whether to participate in their company's 401(k), many people know *exactly* what they want to do before reading a brochure, hearing a sales pitch, or seeing the facts in black and white.

Their answer is "No, because . . ."

> People always think they have a good reason not to join their company plan. Whatever that reason may be, however, it's not good enough. Here are ten of the great excuses—along with the benefits you pass up if you believe them.

Excuse #1: "I can't afford to save for retirement."

Why can't they save? They're *already* saving, for a house . . . for vacation . . . for the kids' education. They don't even have enough right now at the end of the week—where are they going to find the money to save?

I've heard all kinds of people say this—marketing directors

making $150,000, secretaries making $20,000, managers making $45,000, and those with every kind of job and salary you can name. Every person has his or her own variation on this theme.

The fact is that you can't afford *not* to save. Retirement may seem a long way off, particularly if you're under thirty-five, but starting to save early, even in small amounts, will give you a head start that you can't make up for later.

Take a look at the following example. It shows that starting as early as possible, even with a modest amount, can really make a difference—and that it can cost you a substantial amount to play catch-up.

Example: If you start putting away $100 a month when you're twenty-five and stop when you're thirty-five, leaving your account intact until you're sixty-five in an investment earning 8 percent, you'll accrue over $230,000 from an investment of just $13,200. If you wait to start until you're forty-five, you'll have to contribute over $4,500 a year to end up exactly in the same place at sixty-five. But you would have had to contribute over $95,000 to get there!

"Double your money, double your fun . . ." Another advantage of your plan is that your company is likely to match part of your contributions. Most, but not all, companies contribute in some way to their employees' 401(k) accounts. Remember that the only way you'll get this matching money is through your 401(k). You do not have the option of taking it as a cash bonus or in some other lump sum.

Employer matching means one thing: You can make a 100 percent return immediately on the first $1,000 or $2,000 you contribute.

If you can do that well on the rest of your investments, you might have a future as an investment adviser. (Please call me so I can become your client.)

Excuse #2: "It's too hard to understand."

Baloney! Even if you put all your money in what the plan may call a savings account (and most investment advisers would call this just plain nuts), you still do better than you would on your own, because of tax deferral. Why? Because of the taxes you're not paying right now. No taxes on the contributions you're making from your paycheck and no taxes on any of the ways your account is growing.

We already talked about how great compounding is—but combined with tax-deferred saving, it can really shine, because you start out with the largest amount possible. No taxes are due until you start making withdrawals way down the road.

The 401(k) has become so popular in America that the level of education provided to participants like you is likely to be better than in the past. This is because of the competition among companies offering plans to employers. It is also because the Department of Labor (which watches over pension benefits) and/or the Securities and Exchange Commission (SEC) (which oversees the investment community) are looking over the shoulders of plan providers and your company to see that you get enough information to run your account well. While these improvements may not be appearing as quickly as participants want, it's gotten better than it ever was.

Excuse #3: "I don't know how to invest."

No one is asking you to open the business section of the newspaper and pick five stocks on the New York Stock Exchange that will fund your retirement in thirty years. The 401(k) is designed to help you accomplish your long-term saving goals.

Professionally managed funds. Your company's plan will likely offer you several investment options to choose from, unless you're in the small minority that have company-directed investments. The funds are managed by firms that specialize in these kinds of investments (or professionals within your company) and try to increase their value, certainly in line with general market trends and, ideally, better than that.

If you've invested in a mutual fund, it can't do just *anything* with your money. Every fund outlines its investing philosophy in writing, although managers have leeway in following it.

While some funds do better than others, you do have the reassurance of knowing that your money is being handled professionally.

Making a choice. If your plan offers investment choices, it will offer some guidance to help you decide which kinds of investments match your goals and temperament. As I've said, this is called "asset allocation."

Here's more help. Any mutual fund (or similar investment modeled after one) is a diversified investment because it is made up of a variety of stocks and bonds. If you feel that you need additional help in putting together your 401(k)'s portfolio, you probably want to look closely at any "balanced fund," "asset allocation fund," or "lifestyle fund" your plan may offer. (More about this in Chapter 8.)

Of course, this doesn't mean that you don't have to watch how your funds are doing. Even top-performing funds sometimes change investment strategies and never recover from it. Others change managers and take a fall, although this is *not* always the case.

Many plans—even those of big companies—may offer you investment options that do worse than comparable investments or simply do not do well enough against inflation. You can tell them by their poor performance when compared to the market in general or versus similar funds.

Considering the number of mutual funds out there—more than 5,200, with assets of $2.2 trillion—the reason that a company chooses and *sticks with* a loser remains a mystery to me. (I'm not talking about a good fund that has an off year, but a verified stinker.) If your plan offers a fund in a crucial area that is consistently below the performance of others in its category, let your company know that you're aware of it and ask that they look into alternatives.

Excuse #4: "I want to control the way my money is invested."

Do you know so much about investing that you want to do it all yourself? Bravo! Does this mean you shouldn't save through your plan? The answer is no. The benefits—matching, loans, etc.—still are too good to miss. Join, even if you contribute only enough to get your company's maximum matching.

Besides, you might change your job and be able to roll over your money into an IRA at a brokerage firm, where you can put it all in stocks. (Actually, you don't have to leave your job to have this kind of option: You can put up to $2,000 in *after*-tax income into an IRA with a broker and still defer taxes on gains.)

In addition, the latest option being offered to 401(k) participants lets you invest in stocks of your own choosing. It's not yet widely available and not many participants take advantage of it in plans where it is, but things are always changing. If you are interested in this type of option, let your plan administrator (through your benefits department) know.

Read *Money* or *Smart Money* or *Kiplinger's Personal Fi-*

nance, all publications that sometimes carry news specific to 401(k) investors. They can help you find out what's new, so if there are changes being made in the way this type of plan is run, you can ask your company to make changes, too.

Excuse #5: "I don't want to give my company all this money for my retirement."

You're not giving your company anything. The money is still yours, along with any growth that accrues on it. If anything, it's your company that's giving you something: matching funds for part of your contributions. (Remember, if you don't have a 401(k), your boss is not going to give you this money in some other form.) While the matching doesn't automatically become yours from day one, it eventually will.

Most plans will also let you borrow from your savings—usually up to 50 percent of your balance but no more than $50,000—at low rates. However, some plans require you to repay the loan before you can start adding new money to the account.

Excuse #6: "My company has its own pension plan."

If this is true, you're one of the lucky ones, but you're still going to have to supplement that company pension (a "defined benefit" plan) with your own savings—unless you're the head honcho—so they might as well be tax-deferred savings.

Since most pensions don't have cost-of-living adjustments, they actually shrink in value over time by the rate of inflation (at least 3 percent to 4 percent every year). That's why so many companies with pension plans add a 401(k)—to help you do your part in the best way possible.

Excuse #7: "My husband saves at work."

If you're a woman reading this, I have a few questions for you: Do you know how much your husband's pension is? Its survivor provisions? Do you know that your marriage will last? What will your own Social Security account pay you?

Statistics all show that women get shortchanged in the retirement world. This happens, in part, because so many either have had lower-paying jobs, worked part time, or worked only in the home (which doesn't even count as a full-time job for an IRA, no matter how hard you work). Statistics also show that less than one-third of women save for retirement, as compared with about half of men. Women also start later and tend to invest more conservatively—which is not a combination destined for significant growth.

The fact that women usually outlive men makes it even more important to start looking at your own 401(k) if you are part of the work force (or your husband's if you aren't) and do something about joining and contributing the maximum as early as possible.

Excuse #8: "I don't want my money locked up for years."

Why not? How else are you going to have that nest egg when you need it? We all have our good reasons for needing our money elsewhere: We want a new house in order to live a little better, for example—but is it going to double in value in seven years? Don't hold your breath, because those days seem to be gone for the foreseeable future. Keep the mortgage and the 401(k), too.

As for the kids' education, well, this is a delicate subject for everyone, me included. We all want the best for our kids and want them to have more advantages than we had (or at least the same). But look at it this way: Do you want to worry about whether they are going to have the resources to take care of you in your old age? Don't you want to be as independent as possible? Your 401(k) can help you achieve financial independence, if you stick with it.

What can you do to help your kids? Numerous books and magazine articles on the subject of personal finance offer sound, practical techniques for saving for tuition. You can also help your children by helping them secure education loans from a number of sources, or through other forms of support. But please don't mortgage your future.

Excuse #9: "My company should have to pay for retirement."

Amen. I wish that it were possible for everyone to have a company-paid pension. (I wouldn't mind one myself.) But who said life was fair?

Even if your company offers this benefit, if you're like a large part of the boomer generation, you probably haven't worked there long enough to get a large enough pension to live on.

> If you're lucky, you may get small pensions from a couple of your longer-term jobs to add on to your retirement nest egg, but it can't support you, even with some help from Social Security.

If your 401(k) plan has a company-matching provision, this may be as close as you get to your boss's paying for your retirement. Start early enough and this matching can play a real role in making you comfortable later.

Excuse #10: "Social Security will take care of me."

All I have to say about this one is: If you believe that Social Security will take care of all your future needs, you probably believe in the Tooth Fairy, Santa Claus, and the Wizard of Oz.

What You Should Have Learned
from This Chapter

1. Automatic payroll deductions help build your account, because contributions are deposited directly from your paycheck into your plan—before you have a chance to spend the money in some other way.

2. Matching of your contributions by your employer can actually double the value of your money instantly if you have a dollar-for-dollar match. Even if you get just 25 cents or 50 cents for every dollar you contribute, a 25 percent or 50 percent return is better than you can expect from most standard investments.

3. The money you contribute to your 401(k) belongs to you alone, although the company holds on to it for you until you need it. And you can take it with you when you change jobs. (Most plans also let active employees borrow from their accounts—but you should do it only as a last resort.)

4. As a woman eligible to participate in a 401(k), take the opportunity, whether or not you're married, because you're going to need it. Social Security won't take care of all your retirement needs. Neither will a company pension—unless you are president of the company.

5. Your money is unlikely to have the opportunity to grow faster than it will in your 401(k). A house bought today will take until the fifth generation of Star Trek babies to double in value. The days when you could count on your home being a cash cow down the road are gone for good —unless you bought it for a song thirty years ago.

Think About This . . .

Your Top Ten 401(k) Bloopers

10. Not evaluating the number or performance of your plan's investment options—and not speaking up if they leave something to be desired.

9. Trying to second-guess the stock market.

8. Not watching the progress of your investments.

7. Parking all your contributions in a "guaranteed" (GIC) fund.

6. Not taking all the help your plan offers (for example, seminars).

5. Not learning about all your options.

4. Not understanding that your plan is not *saving* but *investing*.

3. Not contributing as much as you can to your plan.

2. Not starting as early as you can.

1. Not joining your plan.

PART II

Getting Started Quickly: Terms to Know, Goals to Think Over, and Choices to Prepare For

4

Setting Out on the Right Foot: A Quick Course for Beginning (or Rethinking) Your Account

The information in this chapter is specially designed to help you get started if you have an enrollment meeting to go to right away. But even if you don't, it can help you get the most out of the plan you already have: It can help you figure out whether what you're doing makes sense—and make some changes if it doesn't. The most important information introduced in this chapter will be discussed in depth later in the book; consult the section entitled "How to Use This Book" on page xxi.

Are you enrolling in a plan for the first time? Haven't previously contributed the maximum allowed by law? Feel you need a refresher? Simply need a break from work? No matter what the circumstance, if your company announces an open meeting about your 401(k) plan, make sure you go.

Not going puts you at a distinct disadvantage. To put it concisely, if you don't show your face and hear what they have to say, *you don't know what you don't know.*

But even if you already skipped the meeting, don't miss this chapter!

Getting the Word Out

The outside companies that run these programs for a majority of plans—mutual fund or insurance companies or banks, etc., called "providers"—treat plan enrollment as if they were selling some kind of product.

> In a way, getting you to join a plan is *not* very different from marketing soap or cereal: The providers have to make you aware that it exists, prove that it's worth buying into, and make sure they keep you as a customer.

They use many of the same techniques employed by consumer product companies—colorful posters, flyers (in your pay envelope), balloons, etc.—all stressing the importance of the plan. By all means, pay attention, because any of this promotional material can offer you information worth having!

Your company really does want you to take advantage of the plan, and there's no hidden motive behind it. The only thing that's in it for them is that the most senior people can't make their maximum contribution if a good sampling of people (including secretaries, mailroom clerks, and cafeteria workers, etc.) throughout the organization don't join.

The Downside of Enrollment:
Too Much, Too Soon

Unfortunately, there is a downside to the whole enrollment process for 401(k)s: It often requires that you make decisions before you're really ready.

The learning curve for most people joining a plan doesn't start until *after* they are already in it—and that's too late for properly dealing with the first choices you need to make.

You may be asked to decide right away on how much to save

(that's easy: as much as you can) as well as what kinds of investments to make. Even the pep talk or video at a meeting isn't enough to help you make intelligent decisions so quickly.

So, ideally, you're reading this before you have to make those first decisions, because you have to live with some for longer than others. Remember: Even if your company lets you change your investment options whenever you want, you can only increase the amount you're setting aside once a year.

The Language of the 401(k) Plan

For many reasons—some technical, some legal, some mysterious—the language of your company's 401(k) may seem to be from some other planet. And being introduced to strange vocabulary just as you have to use it only makes things worse. Relax and don't worry about understanding the language of investing. It really isn't so difficult. Here are some key terms that should give you access to the necessary tools for getting your account moving.

Asset classes. Better known as stocks, bonds, money market instruments: in other words, the types of securities owned by your plan's funds.

Asset allocation. This means dividing your contributions among several *asset classes* (see above) to lower the risks that are part of investing. Sometimes known as "not putting all your eggs in one basket." (See **diversification**.)

For example, you might choose to *allocate* 60 percent of your contributions into stock funds, 20 percent into bond funds, and 20 percent into a money market fund or guaranteed investment contract (GIC). These allocations are then translated into investments from your plan. As your 401(k) contribution is subtracted from each paycheck, it is divided according to the percentages you have already chosen for each fund.

Bear market. A period of time when the stock market goes down significantly. (A *bear* is someone who believes the market will go down.)

Bonds. Buying a bond is the equivalent of making a loan to a company or the government (the "debtor") in return for regular interest payments. A corporate bond fund, for example, offered by your plan is made up of bonds in many companies. The debtor agrees to repay the face value of the bond—which may or may not be the amount you paid—at a fixed date. It may be repaid earlier, but no later than the fixed maturity date, unless specific arrangements are made. Most corporate bonds pay interest semiannually, and fund investors are credited with their share of this payment.

Bonds come in three basic maturities, although there will be some variations from bond to bond: Long-term bonds generally mature in twenty to thirty years and are usually very sensitive to changes in interest rates set by the Federal Reserve in Washington. When interest rates go up, these bond values go down. Intermediate-term bonds generally mature in about seven to ten years and are somewhat less sensitive to interest rate changes. Short-term bonds, which usually mature in one or two years, are the most stable but generally pay the lowest interest.

Among the various kinds of bonds that you may come in contact with through your 401(k) are:

- *U.S. Treasury bonds* (Uncle Sam insures the bonds, but *not* the fund they go into)
- *junk bonds* (also called "high yield," because they pay higher interest to compensate for the added risk of investing in companies that may be in less-than-excellent financial condition)
- *international bonds* (issued by foreign-based companies or governments)

Municipal bonds are not used in tax-deferred accounts like 401(k)s or IRAs, since they are already tax free to some degree and pay a lower interest rate to reflect this. Neither are U.S. Savings Bonds, which are so popular as wedding presents because you buy them at half the face value and someone else has to wait until their accrued interest allows them to be redeemed at face value.

Bull market. A period when the stock market goes up significantly. (A *bull* is someone who believes this will happen.)

Company stock. Your company may contribute shares of its stock to your 401(k) as profit sharing or as matching funds, which you probably won't be able to sell until you leave the company. (Note: There are exceptions; see your plan description for details.) Your plan may also offer company stock as one of your investment options.

Many experts consider this to be one of the riskiest investments for a 401(k)—but may be worth it if you determine that your company has a great future. In the case of companies like Pan Am, Eastern Airlines, or Carter Hawley Hale, which all went bankrupt, employees who had company stock got the double whammy, because their pension funds went bust and so did their stock.

Compound interest. This is the process through which your investment gains value at an ever-increasing rate. Its growth is not only based on your original investment, but on getting interest on the interest you've already earned.

Daily valuation. Just what it says: Daily valuation means that your plan's record keeper constantly calculates the value of your investments. When your plan has a voice-response system, you can call up on any day and find out the value of your investment as of the previous day's market closing. Because your fund balances are always current, you may be permitted to switch investment options or change your allocations among several funds whenever you want, if your plan allows frequent changes.

This feature wasn't always available in 401(k)s—and it still isn't from many plans. If your plan still doesn't offer it, ask your benefits department to consider making a change.

Derivatives. A derivative is a financial instrument whose price is "derived" from the price of something else ("the underlying price"), such as interest rates or the price of a commodity like oil. Investing in derivatives has been described as being similar to placing a bet on how one kind of investment will perform relative to some other kind of investment. If the derivative has "bet" that the price of oil to be delivered next year will go up, and it goes down instead, a fund holding the derivative incurs a loss—sometimes a very big one—as some high-profile investors found out in 1994.

Mutual funds invest in derivatives for a number of reasons.

Money market funds, for example, have invested in these risky devices to raise the interest they are able to pay—even though this strategy has been known to backfire. Other funds that invest in stocks in a foreign currency might invest in derivatives to offset the possibility of changes in a currency rate versus the dollar.

Diversification. In investing, this is also known as "not putting all your eggs in one basket" or "spreading the wealth." By not placing all your contributions into a single investment, diversification lowers your risk. Mutual funds are, by their nature, a diversified investment because they are made up of many stocks, bonds, etc.

In your 401(k), diversification goes one step further, because it means not putting all your money in a single fund, whether it's divided among different kinds of stock funds ("aggressive," "international," or "mid-cap") or different kinds of assets (see **asset allocation**).

Dividends. The portion of a company's profits that is paid out to stockholders. When a mutual fund owns a dividend-paying stock, the dividends it receives are paid to the fund's shareholders either in cash or as an additional portion of a share. Not all stocks pay dividends.

Equities. That's *stocks* to you and me, folks.

Fixed-income securities. That's *bonds* to you and me, folks.

Guaranteed investment contract (GIC). A contract issued by an insurance company that pays a fixed rate of interest for a set amount of time. (Banks have them, too, calling them BICs.) A GIC fund, sometimes called a "stable value fund," owns a variety of contracts. The only thing this kind of fund "guarantees" is the interest rate you are getting for the current quarter, which is based on an average of all the contracts bought by your company's fund. They are not insured, but backed only by the financial condition of the institution that issues them. (See Chapter 8 for more.)

This is one of the investment options offered by many plans that gets absolutely no respect—except from plan participants, who sink an inordinately large part of their contributions into this kind of fund. Most experts consider it too conservative—

which means it doesn't have a very good likelihood of high growth.

Income. Dividends or interest paid by stocks or bonds. As a holder of a mutual fund through your 401(k), you usually receive these as additional shares of the same fund, unless you instruct your provider to "sweep" (their word, not mine) the dividends into a different investment option.

Inflation. A decrease in the buying power of your money. If your money is earning 8 percent but inflation is 4 percent, your savings are actually growing at 4 percent (8 percent minus 4 percent). If your money is earning 3 percent but inflation is 4 percent, you're in big trouble.

Interest. A fixed amount paid to holders of bonds, year in and year out, until the face value of the bond is due. When a mutual fund owns bonds, it distributes the interest it receives to the fund's shareholders either in cash or as an additional portion of a share.

Money market fund. This type of investment consists of all kinds of short-term debt. It generally pays a higher rate of interest than banks offer, but it is not guaranteed. Unlike most other mutual funds, these funds try to maintain a constant value (the "net asset value," or NAV) of $1.00 per share, but the interest will go up and down, depending on the rates paid by its current holdings. In theory, you will never end up with less than you contributed, plus any interest it earns.

It sounds very low risk, doesn't it? It's supposed to be. But a number of high-profile money market funds ran into trouble in 1994 because, in order to keep their return up, they invested in *derivatives*. Some of these investments turned out badly; the managers of larger funds stepped in and made up the difference when the NAV threatened to slide below $1.00, to keep investors from losing money. The moral: Nothing is really absolutely, positively "safe" when you invest.

Mutual fund. Your chance to buy into a wide variety of stocks, bonds, money market instruments, other securities, or a combination of these asset classes, in a single, professionally managed investment. As a 401(k) investor, you may use your contributions to purchase shares of mutual funds, or something that is very similar to one—for example, a sub-account from an insurance company.

Net asset value (NAV). The cost of buying a share of a specific mutual fund on a given day before a load or commission is charged.

Return. The profit produced by your fund, less management fees.

Risk. The chance that you're going to lose money in real terms (interest rates go up, the market goes down, the company goes out of business) or from inflation eating away at it because the interest rate you're receiving is lower than the rate of inflation.

Risk-to-age investment concept. Experts believe that the longer you have until retirement, the riskier you can afford to be as an investor. That's because the further you are from cashing in your investments, the longer you can wait out a downturn in their value. So, they tell us, we can afford to choose riskier investments at twenty-five than we would at fifty-five. (Of course, this doesn't take into consideration personal feelings about taking risks [see Chapter 6], no matter what our age.)

Stocks. Shares of ownership in a corporation. Some companies may have two kinds of stock: *common* stock, which is the basic ownership of the company but must wait until all other debts are paid before earning a dividend; and *preferred* stock, which has features of both stocks and bonds, with a fixed dividend that does not depend on profits, making it more stable.

Common stocks have shown the best return of all investments offered by a plan over the long term—averaging 10 to 12 percent over the sixty years from 1929. Stock funds are primarily comprised of stocks, but may also have bonds or money market instruments among their assets.

Sweep. If you invest in stock or bond funds and get interest/dividends and capital gains distributions, your company's plan may allow you to "sweep" them—transfer them automatically—to a different fund. This is designed to be an easy way to further diversify your investment. (See **income**.)

Total return. This is the most common way of measuring the performance of a mutual fund or any other investment. Two components affect total return:

- the *increase in price* of a fund
- any *distributions* that come from either interest/dividends on the securities in the fund's portfolio or the sale of any of
. the fund's holdings at a gain/loss

Total return expresses these two elements as a percentage of the annual gain/loss in the investment's value.

Vesting. The schedule by which you own your company's matching contributions to your 401(k). The most generous companies offer immediate vesting. Usually, it's all yours within five years, with partial ownership increasing annually.

Volatility. The major fluctuations in the value of your investment, which have a lesser effect over time. Funds that invest largely in the stocks of small companies are generally the most volatile in the short term, because of the possibility of a wide swing in price; those investing in Treasury bills are generally the least.

Standard deviation is a measurement of a mutual fund's potential for volatility, according to Lipper Analytical Services, which keeps track of such things. A Ginnie Mae fund (see description in Chapter 8) has a very low standard deviation number, 1.1, because of its low risk; a country or area fund will have a high number, indicating its high risk (Japan funds are at 8.3).

Starting Out

Now that you've begun to get some of the vocabulary under control, you can start to figure out the important things for every successful 401(k) participant to think about, even before enrollment:

- what you want the plan to do for you
- how you're going to accomplish your goal(s)

This is quite a bit to think about, but before you have adequately considered these two points, you may feel pressured to make other important decisions—specifically, your investment choices. Why the push? There are several reasons, but usually it's because the plan provider believes that if you don't make your decisions on the spot, you will:

- not make them at all
- choose to contribute less than the maximum allowed
- put your money in what you consider to be a very safe investment option (and never take it out again).

In short, you might become one of the "ones that got away," thereby making the plan less successful, and providers don't want that to happen.

Preparing to Take Action

You, on the other hand, might have other things in mind—such as talking things over with your spouse, your financial adviser, or someone else who may know a thing or two about investing.

So, what do you do? The first thing you have to figure out is where you want to go—a goal. Obviously, your primary goal is to provide the best nest egg you can for retirement. In order to accomplish this feat, there are three questions you need to address:

What is this plan and what is it designed to do for me?

You should have a good idea of your goals by now: The 401(k) is a long-term investing plan that is designed to help you pay for retirement. It is *not* designed to help you buy a beach house or a Cadillac or a trip to Hawaii.

How much risk am I willing to accept?

This may be the most important question you ask yourself in the context of being an investor. Risk, as defined earlier in the chapter, is the possibility that you are going to lose money. Can you

live with this uncertainty? Well, don't be in too much of a hurry
to label yourself a "low-risk investor."

I once heard an expert say that if you have no grief while investing through your 401(k), you'll have nothing but grief when
you retire—because you probably have been too conservative
to accumulate a large enough nest egg.

There's no such thing as a risk-free investment—but the rewards of investing *may* be worth the risk. (More about this in
Chapter 6.) I emphasize the word *may*. Only you can decide
what level of risk you can live with. Most people don't want to
wake up at 3 A.M., worrying about what the stock market in
Hong Kong is doing. Some, however, find that exciting.

You shouldn't worry about every fluctuation in the value of
your account; in the framework of a *long-term investing strategy,* the majority of investment professionals agree that these
kinds of concerns are not really important.

If you put all your money in an ultraconservative investment
to "protect" yourself, though, you should consider carefully
what you are giving up way down the road: the chance for a
more comfortable future.

What kind of investment mix can I
live with—and stick with?

Deciding on the kinds of investments that will help you make
your 401(k) grow to its maximum is, I admit, no easy task, but
it's not impossible, either.

As I said in the glossary above, your age is one indication of
how much risk you should be able to tolerate. A twenty-five-
year-old investor has time on his or her side for letting the benefits of long-term investing and compounding do their best
work. But even at fifty-five—or sixty-five—you can have a significant time frame ahead of you for stocks to boost your plan

account. After all, you could live another twenty to thirty years! (See Chapter 7 for a complete discussion of this topic.)

Top choices. If you feel ready to choose your investment options, that's great. Here's a brief description of the five types of funds most frequently offered by plans, according to one survey:

- a **money market account** (a low-risk, low-return kind of fund)
- a **stable income fund** (a kind of savings account)
- a **balanced fund** (mixing stocks, bonds, and money market securities)
- a **stock index fund** (which is comprised of all the stocks in an index such as the Standard & Poor's 500, one of the major benchmarks of stock performance)
- a **stock fund** (a mixture of stocks, generally of larger companies, chosen by your plan's investment manager)

A balanced approach? If you haven't invested before and feel timid about doing so, the people running your meeting may encourage you to consider a "balanced" fund—or the "lifestyle"/ "asset allocation" funds (mentioned earlier in the book). You may feel this will take the worry out of putting together a diversified portfolio, but don't count on it. (See Chapter 7.)

Being more aggressive. No matter how conservative you consider yourself, the experts agree that you will want *something* that's aggressive for at least part of your investment (that is, some type of stock fund), to get a better long-term return from your contributions.

Of course, as you can see from the list of popular types of funds above, none is marked AGGRESSIVE! or DANGER! So there's a fair likelihood that you won't even see a higher-risk option in your plan. I would be neglectful if I didn't mention, however, that there are an awfully large number of people who do very well investing in funds that could be categorized as highly risky. These include very aggressive small company funds, whose performance can be a roller-coaster ride even when providing a very high average return. Many investors in these kinds of funds live to tell the tale—of higher balances in their accounts.

Six Tips for Getting Off on the Right Foot (or Getting Back to It)

There's no sense in being part a 401(k) if you don't get as much as you can out of it, as soon as you can. Here are a few things to think about and do:

Tip #1: Stop, look, and listen.

Educational techniques are getting more sophisticated in showing the features of the plan as well as simplifying the mysteries of investing.

The best of them will also give you hints for finding money to save that you didn't know you had—or getting more out of what you do save. (For instance, if you've taken a second job to put aside money for a nest egg, you'd be better off spending the additional income on everyday expenses and saving through your primary job's 401(k).) The more sophisticated providers may have interactive computer models and lively videos that can actually make learning about your plan interesting. Others may provide less stimulating presentations that make you work harder to get at the information they have to give.

Even if you're not interested in going to a meeting, you may be able to get a video from your benefits office that can help you take charge of your account. Borrow one, pop it into your VCR—and invite your spouse to watch it with you.

Tip #2: Fill out a form.

Yes, sign up to participate and contribute as much as you can. No, don't make an investment choice until you have to. (See Tip

#3.) Go home and talk it over with an adviser or your spouse or with a friend who knows something about investing.

Tip #3: Evaluate the features.

See how flexible the plan is—in particular, whether it has *daily valuation.* If it does, and you can make changes in your account frequently, making your first choices seem less life-or-death. You can, for example, park your money in a fund with low risk and modest return until you figure out what investments you really want to make.

If, however, you can make changes only a couple of times a year, your first choice of funds is extra important. So insist that you are not ready to choose, and find out how long you really have until your allocations *must* be made.

Remember: It's a rare plan that's not worth joining to get the maximum company matching.

Tip #4: Glance at investment information.

In general, if your plan's investments are among the mutual fund listings in the newspaper, they will come with a prospectus—a little booklet that describes the fund's past performance, the kinds of investments it makes, and other things. The most useful information will probably be about **performance**—how it has done over the last year, three years, five years, life of fund, etc. (Unfortunately, with other investments, you may be given much less information.)

The Securities and Exchange Commission, which regulates the stock and bond markets, has mandated that all mutual fund materials carry a disclaimer to the effect that "past performance is no guarantee of future results," and you'll probably see the same line in any 401(k) investment material. The funds say this, but they really would like you to think that the golden age of this particular fund, which has (for example) paid 17 percent over the last five years, will continue. They need the disclaimer just in case it doesn't. The fact is that past performance is about the best basis you have for choosing among your fund's options. (See Chapter 8 for more on the prospectus.)

Tip #5: Choose among your options.

Don't jump into a stock fund that could hold you hostage during what could be a prolonged "bear market," when the stock market is being nervous about whether the economy is too strong *or* too weak and is going down, down, down. (Who said the markets make any sense?) It's better to pick a low-risk fund as a temporary haven than to make uninformed decisions.

On the other hand, if you do know what you're doing, you might as well start your money working for you as hard as it can right away. (See Chapter 7 for more about investments.)

Tip #6: Don't make yourself crazy.

As I said earlier, try not to let yourself be overwhelmed by the thought of how much you're told you will need forty years from now. You can't do more than you can.

PART III

Taking Charge: Becoming an Investor, Handling Risk, and Evaluating Your Options

5

Yes, You *Can* Be an Investor!

In this chapter I'll tell you about the tools that are available to you in teaching yourself how to be an investor instead of a saver—and why this is so important in getting the most out of your 401(k) plan. It's not as hard as you think—and you may even find that you enjoy it!

Before we get started, here are a few questions to think about.

DO YOU KNOW . . . ?

. . . whether each of these statements is true or false?

1. A mutual fund gives you access to a basketful of securities with a single purchase.

      TRUE _____   FALSE _____

2. Timing is everything in the stock market.

      TRUE _____   FALSE _____

3. Most 401(k) participants want to make their own investment decisions.

      TRUE _____   FALSE _____

4. Most 401(k) participants *feel qualified* to make their own investment decisions.

      TRUE _____   FALSE _____

5. There are people who are *born* investors and others who *learn* to be investors.

      TRUE _____   FALSE _____

ANSWERS:

1. True. While a mutual fund can make large purchases of stock in a few companies, most of its money (75 percent) has to be spread around so that it owns no more than 5 percent of any single security.

2. False. You have a very small chance of timing buying or selling to take advantage of the ups and downs of the stock market.

3. True. Research has shown that 401(k) participants want to take responsibility for their investment decisions.

4. False. Research has also shown that these participants feel unprepared to take on this responsibility.

5. True. Yes, it's true that some people are born with the instincts that make them successful in the world of stocks and bonds—but you can also teach yourself to be an investor. In this chapter you'll learn how to start.

As a 401(k) participant, you're not the first person to be suddenly thrust, head first, into the unknown waters of the investing world.

Not long ago, millions of people who used to put their savings in CDs found that this was no longer giving them much bang for their bucks. What did they do? They headed for mutual funds, where, with a single purchase, they could get a basketful of stocks or bonds, chosen and managed by a professional.

What's the Difference?

Did most of them understand the difference between buying a bank certificate of deposit, where the only risk is inflation, and a mutual fund, which is open to all kinds of risks (to be discussed shortly)? It's highly unlikely. This lack of knowledge didn't hold them back, but you can do better for yourself if you choose *not* to stay in the dark about investing.

You *can*—in fact, you must—teach yourself how to be an investor, because you are responsible for being able to tell whether your plan account is on track or needs a change.

It doesn't mean spending hours a day reading *The Wall Street Journal* (although it's not as intimidating as it may sound). It just takes a little effort that *any*one can make.

Who's Smarter than You?

> Do you have the feeling that everyone else knows more about investing than you do? Be comforted with the thought that it's just not true—and that you're not the only one who feels this way.

There are hundreds of thousands of people—cutting right across every income and educational level—who are sure that they are "the only one" not savvy about investing. No matter what their IQs, no matter how successful they are at their careers, they peg themselves as "conservative" and incapable of investing their money, except in the simplest, least risky of ways—for example, in a bank CD.

These feelings of insecurity have kept many of them from joining their 401(k)s or, if they do join, from choosing any option more risky than the plan equivalent of a savings account. On the other hand, even more *have* joined in spite of these feelings and have learned how to overcome them and become investors.

You can, too.

One of the surprise best-selling books of 1995 was *The Beardstown Ladies' Common-Sense Investment Guide* (Hyperion Books). It tells the story of a group of women in Illinois who started their own investment club and have "outpaced and outclassed most other devotees of the stock market." None was an investment professional, but all followed the club's guiding principles: financial enrichment, enjoyment, and (my emphasis) *education.*

The Long-Term Outlook

Are you reluctant to take on these responsibilities? You're not alone. *Most of us are scared to death of investing.* After all, investments aren't insured. Isn't it better to protect our nest eggs from the *unknown?* The answer, simply, is NO.

Indeed, you and I aren't the only ones worrying about how unprepared we are to deal with the investment markets. There have been dire predictions that newcomers to the investment arena—including many of us 401(k) participants—are going to lead to the eventual collapse of the securities and mutual fund markets because they don't understand the risk of their investments.

"Past Performance Is No Guarantee of Future Results"

One day, say some "experts," there will be a bump in the markets and the sudden mass withdrawals by inexperienced investors will cause the biggest stock market crash in history.

Why would this happen? Because, they believe, these investors commonly disregard one of the most important statements in every prospectus, 401(k) plan description, and mutual fund sales brochure. It reminds us all that no matter how good an investment's performance has been in the past, there is no guarantee that it will continue to act in the same way. These experts also believe that, while investors have heard the expression "What goes up comes down," they don't really believe it refers to their own investments.

No Catastrophes Yet

This catastrophe hasn't happened yet. In fact, it's very often professionals who cause stock market gyrations: On January 15,

1995, for example, *The Wall Street Journal* reported on stock market response to the Mexican peso's devaluation: "It isn't the small investor who is spooked. It is the pros."

Even in 1994, which was a pretty bad time in the stock market, withdrawals from mutual funds, including 401(k)s and IRAs, were not massive in comparison with the number of mutual fund shares purchased in the previous year. (Of course, deposits did not increase at the rate they had a year earlier, but why would they?)

And withdrawals in reaction to market turbulence won't be enormous, if small investors—including you and me—remember the most important thing about investing in stocks and stock funds: It's long term. Over the last sixty years or so, stocks have produced an average annual return of more than 10 percent, but there were many ups and downs—and some real roller-coaster rides—along the way.

While there is always the risk of losing money, the longer you leave your stock market investments untouched, the more time they will have to grow in value.

Timing Is Not Everything

It is important to remember this as well: Stock market data has shown that timing is *not* everything. There have been very few people who got in and out of the market just at the right times to make a real difference in their investment outcomes. If you take away all the bear markets—which produce a big sell-off and depressed stock prices—of the last sixty years, their effects on long-term investments would not be all that significant, a difference of about one-half of 1 percent in the total return.

T. Rowe Price, the big mutual fund company and 401(k) provider, did a test to see what the impact of timing really is. Using the period between 1969 and 1989, it tested the result of investing $2,000 a year into the stocks of the S&P 500. If you did it on the day the stocks were at their highest for each calendar year, the average annual rate of return was 11.4 percent; if you invested when it was lowest for the year, you did much better,

13.5 percent. Yes, there's a difference—but not worth panicking about.

Getting Advice

Over the last few years, there has been lots of research around showing that 401(k) participants want to make their own investment decisions but don't feel qualified to do so; they want the tools to do a better job of running their retirement plans.

Things are definitely improving. These days, egged on by the Department of Labor and the SEC, most 401(k) providers will give you lots of information that is supposed to help you "do it yourself." It's true that the vast majority of mutual fund and insurance companies and banks are still not prepared to sit you down and give the individualized investment advice that so many participants would welcome. (Many companies do everything short of telling you which specific investments are the best ones for you, however.)

Why? The SEC has certain rules about how well an investment adviser must know your needs before he or she makes a recommendation. (They must also lower their management fees if they suggest you buy their own funds.) Your company, the plan sponsor, is also nervous about getting too involved in helping you to make choices that might give them liability down the road for bad investment performance. Still, upper-income employees at some companies have been getting additional personal financial planning services thrown in as one of their benefits for quite some time. Benefits consultants report that this kind of help has begun trickling down to employees at all levels.

For the most part, though, if you want investment advice, you have to find yourself an independent investment adviser. There are a few companies, such as IBM, that actually give employees an allowance to be used for contacting an outside financial consultant about their 401(k) investments.

When I was faced with my first 401(k) plan, nobody was particularly interested in holding my hand when it came to understanding some pretty basic matters about:

- Why pick stocks versus bonds?
- What's important in the prospectus?
                    and
- What's "asset allocation" and how do you do it?

It was "everybody into the pool"—and it didn't matter whether I could swim or not. And I couldn't. While it's true I didn't go to the open meeting about the plan, I couldn't find anyone who had—and no benefits person ever followed up on it. When I asked my boss his strategy, he proudly said all his contributions were going to the "guaranteed" option, "so I don't have to think about it." (That's what he thought. See Chapter 8 on GIC funds.)

Just Say No—and Take Control

What did I do? I did what many other people in the same boat as I have done—I just said "NO" to following the uninformed crowd and decided to change my life.

Where did I start? By beginning to educate myself—because before you start taking action, you need the information to make sure your action makes sense.

Here's how I did it. I started with the kinds of things I felt comfortable doing. While it might not be the right plan for everyone, it should start you thinking about your own strategy.

Magazines and newspapers. Mainly, I read. Magazines, newspapers, newsletters—anything I could get my hands on. There are lots of them out there. (That put me in another spot, of course: Who you gonna trust?) My first choice was *Money,* which is the mother of all personal finance magazines. It presents the beginning investor with information in a clear, concise style. If you've never seen it, believe me, you don't need to be a nuclear physicist to read it (and it may give you useful suggestions about other aspects of your financial life).

When I started out, I made sure I read it cover to cover each month. Not everything was important to me, but I at least skimmed every article. Later, I added *Kiplinger's Personal Fi-*

nance, Your Money, Worth, and *Smart Money.* Since these magazines are monthlies (*Your Money* is bimonthly), don't expect to find any hot tips that will make you a million overnight. On the other hand, you *will* read about trends that have a longer life span.

The worst problem with personal finance publications is that they have to come up with exciting new stories every month. Cover stories about "The Five Best Funds to . . ." may seem to offer choices that contradict each other from one issue to another.

Also, today's "hot" investment strategy can get cold very fast—and a monthly magazine's deadlines don't give editors the chance to report on quickly changing trends.

I also was lucky enough to have *The New York Times* as my local newspaper, although, until recently, they chose to highlight personal finance on the day when readership is lowest (Saturday); now they, too, have decided to beef up their coverage in response to the role that personal finance must play in all our lives, and highlight it in the main business section on Sundays. Even *The Wall Street Journal* can be surprisingly accessible if you give it a chance.

While *Business Week* and *Fortune* aren't specifically for investors and (particularly the latter) may be overly geared toward the options open to high-salary individuals to be of interest to most new investors, they can give some insight into personal investing issues.

You don't have to subscribe to all these publications yourself. Look for them at your local or company library, through computer services like America Online, or even in your company lounge. If you can't find them, ask if they can be ordered for general use.

Television and radio. I also watched TV—fighting my kids to get to *Wall Street Week* or *New Jersey Nightly News* on PBS or any number of shows on cable's CNBC (the Dolans, for example) instead of Bullwinkle or the Mighty Morphin Power Rangers. And I kept an ear out during breakfast to hear what the business news had to say on radio.

For immediacy, nothing can beat TV and radio—something happens and you hear about it on the spot. This, of course, has its downside as well, since reporting today seems to be more about tragedy than giving information. Thus, you're most likely to hear immediately, "The Dow is down," "Interest rates are up," and lots of other news like "The middle class is rioting in Brazil because of high interest rates caused by crushing foreign debt" (an actual quote), which can be jarring, to say the least, although not necessarily meaningful.

Ads. Here's another thing I did—and it should make big mutual fund advertisers (who spend big bucks to blow their own horns in magazines and newspapers) very happy: I also read the ads of mutual fund companies. They are a great source of information, and as I've said, information is what learning to invest is all about.

What do they give you? Well, you don't get too many fund specifics because mutual fund companies are too busy worrying about the SEC's reaction to their ad copy. What we end up with are facts that the SEC can't dispute—but that aren't necessarily meaningful to investment decisions.

Funds are very quick to say that they have "Four Stars" or are "Rated #1," but may leave out a few relevant details. In April '95, for example, many stock fund ads proclaimed a "top" one-year return that was mainly based on a great first quarter of '95. They didn't mention the negligible or negative return for most of '94.

But you *can* get some general information from ads. For instance, Vanguard uses pie charts in its ads to show how retirement investments could be divided among different options for different results at different stages of your life. And a number of companies have ads that show the benefits of investing part of your money in international stocks versus U.S.-only stocks, with numbers to back them up.

> All the major mutual fund firms also offer toll-free numbers to call for booklets, worksheets, and asset allocation formulas that are useful in learning more about investing. Most materials are free and arrive quickly.

Talk to your friends. Do you know who among your friends and colleagues has more than a passing interest in investing? It may surprise you. It might surprise you even more what bits of wisdom they have to pass on to you. This doesn't mean, of course, that you should take everything they have to say at face value. But it may raise some issues, answer some questions, or give you some suggestions that make your own quest for knowledge a little easier.

Books? You may have noticed I haven't mentioned books. If you have one of the warehouse-style bookstores near you, you'll notice the shelves are brimming with books by professionals espousing their own philosophy of investing. While some of them may be good reading, few are worth the price of admission. The series of books that includes *Personal Finance for Dummies* (IDG Books) comes closest to giving the nonprofessional investor something to use that is not too intimidating. Yet it, too, fails to give you much specific information on 401(k)s.

Beware of books that try to cover a broad topic like personal finance in too little space; this usually means that they pick and choose which subjects to highlight, covering some in too much detail, leaving others out completely, and sometimes are misleading because of it.

Other Sources

There are additional sources of information about investing that you should know about, although all do not provide free tools. The Investment Company Institute (P.O. Box 27850, Washington, D.C. 20038-7850), a trade association for over 5000 mutual funds, offers a number of free publications, including *What is a Mutual Fund?* and *Investing: Start Now.* The Mutual Fund Education Alliance (1900 Erie St., Suite 120, Kansas City, MO 64116), a smaller trade organization, has an Investor's Series Education Kit for $15, which includes an hour-long audio tape on how to direct your own mutual fund investments, geared toward beginners. Finally, you might consider joining the American Association of Individual Investors (625 N. Michigan Ave., 19th fl., Chicago, IL 60611), which, while expensive at $49, offers good materials and access to local groups where you can meet other investors.

Becoming an Investment Genius?

Remember, you don't have to become an investment genius—I figured out what to do with my account and you can, too. But you might surprise yourself and actually *like* investing—and learn to be more than just "good" at it.

> What you may find interesting is that there are lots of everyday folks who turn out to be better than the professionals at choosing their investments.

In fact, a *Business Week* cover story about individual investors—as they put it, "rank amateurs who have beaten the pros at the toughest game on Wall Street"—was a good lesson in what confidence can do for you and how you don't have to follow the advice of the pros to make it. It found that many of these people have become successful self-taught investors by simply following their own feelings and using a little trial and error.

For example, some "amateurs" don't believe in diversifying or that growth stocks are *only* for younger investors who have time for their stocks to bounce back.

> When it comes to investing, it seems, *anything that works for you* is a reasonable strategy.

Many of them followed the same television programs and publications I mentioned above, while they also added some more specialized media that are more suitable for investors interested in individual stocks (for example, *Investor's Business Daily* or *Barron's*) rather than in mutual funds.

You'll find similar success stories in *Money* about "regular" people out there who have been beating the odds and making themselves over into investors to be reckoned with. In addition, *The Wall Street Journal* runs stories every three months to show how the predictions of the professionals fare against darts thrown haphazardly against the stock market pages—and the pros don't always win.

Peter Lynch, the financial champ who used to head the Fidelity Magellan Fund, says in his book, *Beating the Street* (Simon & Schuster, 1993), that he believes there are plenty of amateurs who can beat the pros by doing their homework and studying the performance of the companies that they plan to invest in. Not every expert shares his opinion—after all, it might put them out of business!—but Lynch has a pretty good record for being right.

Do You Need a Financial Planner?

There is one more thing that you *may* want to do for yourself: find a professional to help you decide among your investment options. Yes, it will cost you money, but many people believe it is worth having a financial planner eyeball your plan's choices, particularly if you have a large number of funds to choose from and feel personally unable to put together a plan. (When it comes to taking your money *out* of the plan, an adviser may be even more important.) On the other hand, most people who haven't chosen to use a planner for other aspects of their financial life don't usually use one for their 401(k).

Financial planners are paid in several ways: for example, by the size of your account, if you are giving them money to manage, or from the commission on certain funds. But since you'll be limited to the funds offered by your plan, you should find a "fee only" planner, who derives income from fees alone, being paid by the hour (average: $150 an hour) or a specific fee (with specifically outlined services included), and not for recommending specific investments.

According to *Money* magazine, there are more than 250,000 advisers calling themselves financial planners or consultants. Included in this number are many not officially licensed to give this type of assistance to you, although many stockbrokers or insurance agents may be capable of giving you valid advice.

You might try to find a financial planner registered with the SEC, although this is no guarantee that you will be ultimately delighted with your choice. (Since 1980, the number of financial planning firms registered with the SEC has risen to 17,500, and they don't have the resources to check up on every one of them.) The SEC requires that they tell you in writing of their experience and education. (You can look into their backgrounds through the SEC's Public Reference Branch, Stop 1-2, 450 Fifth Street NW, Washington, D.C. 20549; 202-418-0270.)

How do you find a good financial planner? Probably through a satisfied referral, although, again, this does not guarantee that you'll be happy, too.

There are trade organizations you can check with for referrals in your area: The Institute of Certified Financial Planners (800-

282-7526), The American Institute of Certified Public Accountants' Personal Financial Planning Division (800-862-4272), and the National Association of Personal Financial Advisers (fee only) (708-537-7722) are good places to start.

What kinds of questions should you ask, besides how are they compensated and whether they are SEC-registered? Make sure to inquire about the type of clients they have, and whether any are similar to you in terms of investment goals.

When it comes down to actually making a choice among several planners who seem competent to help you, your own feelings about them should be your final guide.

The one thing you should *not* do is give a planner the right to make ongoing changes in your account unless you belong to one of the few 401(k)s that actually offer this option to participants. There's a scam being run by some so-called professionals to whom participants pay a fee and authorize to use the voice-response system and their PIN number to switch funds and allocations. Next thing they know, their accounts have been run into the ground. Who's responsible? Ultimately, you are.

Watch Those Investments!

One thing never changes for anyone in a 401(k): You're never off the hook about watching your investments. You don't have to read the financial pages every day or even every week, but neither can you sit back and let "somebody else" do all the worrying. You have to look things over on an ongoing basis, say, at least a couple of times a year.

No investment takes care of itself—in effect, you have to become the "manager" of your portfolio, to make sure that your investment choices are performing the way they should. Even if you have limited control of your account, you need to know whether your investments are performing satisfactorily versus the competition, in order to question your company about them.

This means taking responsibility for doing a couple of things:

Watching your returns. Your plan should provide you with a few figures that you need to monitor carefully.

- **each fund's annual return**—so you can see how you did in real terms and which other plan funds may be doing better.
- **a benchmark for evaluating the annual return**—usually the S&P 500, which you can find in the business section of your newspaper or in the quarterly roundups of mutual funds in personal finance magazines. Are you doing better or worse? If it's much worse, you should find out why. (Much better? Just be grateful!)
- **return over time**—how has it done for the last three, five, and ten years? How has it done versus the (for example) S&P 500 for that period?

Are you where you want to be? If not, think about what to do, but remember to look further than the current quarter.

Switching funds. While acknowledging that investing through your 401(k) is a long-term investment, no one ever promised that your first choices would be your last. You may be unhappy with the way a certain fund has performed after seeing it go down when the rest of the market was going up. It may be time to reconsider the factors that led you to choose a fund in the first place. (See Chapter 7 on asset allocation.)

You will also need to decide when to say "enough is enough" and pull the plug on a bad choice. How long is "enough"? According to Peter Lynch, who managed the Fidelity Magellan Fund during the years it produced the best return of any mutual fund ever, three years is a good length before you dump a fund. You might not have this much patience—I'd say two—but remember, the short-term risk in stocks can be sky-high.

Rebalancing. Rebalancing your account simply means bringing it back to your original intentions. If you chose a fifty-fifty mix of stocks and bonds, and a great year in the stock market increased that part of your portfolio so you now have 60 percent of your account balance in stocks, you may want to consider transferring some of the money now in your stock fund into bonds. Alternatively, you may want to increase your risk factor and leave it more heavily weighted toward stocks.

And the Winner Is . . .

With the kinds of help I discussed in this chapter, I believe that you can get and stay on the road to a better retirement. You might even do better than just "all right"—but it probably means not keeping all your money in what appear to be conservative investments (and may not be) and to become part of the stock market.

What You Should Have Learned
from This Chapter

1. Don't think that everyone else knows more about being an investor than you, because it's just not true. You *can teach* yourself to be an educated participant in today's stock and bond markets—and you have to, to do the best for your 401(k).

2. Investing for retirement is a long-term commitment. Don't reach for your plan's telephone hotline every time the market starts to go down. The experts agree that timing is *not* everything and that you risk getting lower returns by trying to outguess the markets. Professionals don't always get it right, either.

3. The information that you get from most 401(k) plans isn't everything you need to make your investment decisions. Your company and the company that runs your plan don't want to get involved in giving specific investment advice for a variety of reasons.

4. Start reading magazines like *Money, Kiplinger's Personal Finance, Worth, Your Money,* or *Smart Money.* They can help you learn about the world of investing. You may be able to get them at your local library or in the company lounge. If they're not available, ask for them to be ordered for you and others like you.

5. Can you really become good at investing? You would not be the first. *Business Week*'s cover story on "rank amateurs who beat the professionals" or the success of the Beardstown Ladies' investment club are revelations for all of us. You may be surprised who knows about investing—ask your friends.

6

Risky Business: How to Deal with Risk

In this chapter we'll discuss risk—because there's more risk involved in being an investor than losing some of your money in a stock market crash. You'll learn about evaluating your own taste for risk, including what to do when the markets are volatile.

First, a few questions for you to think about.

DO YOU KNOW . . . ?

. . . which of the following opposites is the riskier thing to do? (Check only one of each pair.)

1. Being too conservative in investments? or too aggressive? _____

2. Having too many investments? or too few? _____

3. Changing investment options too often? or never changing at all? _____

4. Contributing too little? or starting too late? _____

5. Not joining at all? or joining with plans to spend it now? _____

ANSWERS:

Neither statement in numbers 1, 2, 3, and 5 is the absolutely less risky alternative. Each alternate has its own specific downside, if taken on its own. The idea is to find a balance between the two extremes. In number 4, starting too late is definitely more risky—because time can make even a little grow very large in a 401(k). This chapter will discuss what's bad—and what's good—about risk.

> All risks worth taking have at least one thing in common: the promise of a payoff for holding your breath and giving it a try. You have to be aware from the start, of course, that the exhilaration of success could end in the agony of defeat, but that shouldn't stop you from trying.

What kinds of risk have you dreamed about taking? Scaling a mountain? Riding a raft down rapids? Getting married (again)?

Most people don't think that it's "in their blood" to make a killing in the stock market. It's for Rockefellers or Kennedys. Even if you make a few bucks on a stock, that's all it will be—because who has enough money to invest $50,000 or $100,000? That's when you really make a killing, right? When you have *real* money to invest. Right?

In my house, about the only thing I ever heard about investing was that my parents invested some of my brother's college money in a mutual fund—and lost every last cent in one of the great mutual fund debacles of the 1960s. That was that. And when I was in sixth grade, my class had to choose a couple of stocks and watch them. Ford was one of my choices. If I'd bought some shares back in those days, I'd be sitting pretty today. (But I didn't and I'm not.)

But it's not just someone else's concerns that make us cautious. I don't remember the big market plunge that took place in 1973, but, thank you, the memories of 1987's dive or the contortions that went on through most of 1994 are enough to provide some awfully potent affirmation of the calm nature it takes to be in the stock market.

Why Deal with Risk at All?

If there's anything guaranteed to make you think about being a more aggressive investor, it should be the alternatives: Would you prefer a savings account whose interest rate doesn't keep up with inflation—so you see your account's real value shrink every day? Do you want to put your future in the hands of the Social Security system?

Many first-time investors who started out scared to death have found that they can do it—and, even better, that they like it. They understand that opportunity to earn higher returns on their money by investing—and the risk that goes along with it—is something that they must learn to live with if they are to get where they want to go (for example, to Florida, Arizona, Spain, or Mexico).

I mentioned earlier the shift from "saving" to "investing." Why has this been necessary? Because of the granddaddy of all risks: **inflation.**

Inflation is what changes the money you save in your mattress into just plain lumps—because it eats away at money's buying power year by year.

Here are the average returns from various kinds of investments over the past forty years—with and without counting inflation:

	Return	*After Inflation*
Large company stock	10.3%	7%
Small company stock	12.4%	9%
Corporate bonds	5.6%	2.4%
Long-term government bonds	5%	1.8%
Intermediate-term government bonds	5.3%	2.1%
Treasury bills	3.9%	.5%

Pretty dramatic, don't you think?

What Lies in Front of You

Say inflation rises at an average rate of 4 percent a year. A loaf of bread that costs $1.00 today will cost

$1.04 next year
$1.08 the year after
$1.12 the year after
$1.17 the year after
$1.22 the year after
$1.27 the year after
$1.32 the year after
$1.37 the year after
$1.42 the year after
$1.48 in 10 years

While that may not seem all that much taken one dollar at a time, if you think of it in terms of hundreds or thousands of dollars, it becomes quite a different story:

You're going to need to increase the value of your savings by 50 percent just to stay in the same place. And as we all know, even when they say that "inflation is running at about 3 percent" (as it was at the start of 1995), we're really the ones who are doing the running.

Maybe it was the price of steel that went up so little; everything we buy as consumers seems to go up much more than that. When the price of a postage stamp went up at the start of 1995, from 29¢ to 32¢, for example, that was more than a 10 percent increase; my Sunday newspaper just went from $2.00 to $2.50—a whopping 25 percent.

Running in Place—or Worse

At the same time the government reported that the inflation rate was just under 3 percent, the statement from my commercial bank showed a savings account interest rate of 2.60 percent. (Checking was paying 1.25 percent!) I was bleeding slowly but surely.

Research shows 401(k) investors to be extremely conservative, with the youngest contributors easily the most gun-shy. Their first choice is the equivalent of an old friend, the savings account; the option may be called a GIC or "stable" fund.*

Although they currently pay half of what they did at their peaks in the eighties, GIC funds still account for a very significant (though declining) portion of all money going into 401(k)s. As higher interest rates have begun to make a comeback, combined with a more volatile stock market, these kinds of accounts have become more appealing again. For the first time in years, their rates have equaled or bettered the returns of many mutual funds.

Over the long term, however, GIC funds aren't the place to put the bulk of your 401(k) contributions if you plan to comfortably beat the rate of inflation. (More on this Chapter 7.)

False Security

Keeping your money in some kind of savings account opens you up to what is called "inflation-related risk"—risk that looks as if it is protecting the money you originally invested/deposited (the "principal") but is really giving you a false sense of security.

---

*It could have been worse—for example, a lower-paying, but perhaps less risky, money market fund.

Why? Because your account isn't growing fast enough to outrun inflation, which is often called "the silent thief," since it steals away your buying power when you're not looking.

Here's an example of what inflation does to money that is not growing fast enough. Say you take the $10 you were going to spend on underwear and instead put it in a savings account paying 3 percent. You think that you are being responsible and conservative and pat yourself on the back. A year later, you decide you need to make the purchase after all and take the $10-plus-interest out of your account. Even though it seems as though your money is still there and growing, something is different: While you weren't looking, inflation has been growing at 3.5 percent—and you actually have $10.30* to buy something that now costs $10.35. You've lost buying power—which is what inflation is all about.

Other Kinds of Risk

There's no doubt that *risk* is probably the most feared word that new investors have to deal with, because it comes in so many shapes and sizes. Everyone has to deal with the risk of inflation, whether they invest or not. As an investor, however, there are special risks to keep in mind. For example:

- the risk that interest rates will go up or down, because stock and, particularly, bond prices are affected by interest rates (as many investors learned in 1994)
- the risk that a particular fund will go down in price because one of its big holdings fails
- the risk that the whole stock market will be depressed

Nobody likes to think of him- or herself as taking an unnecessarily risky position with regard to any of these possibilities. *Smart Money,* the personal finance magazine of *The Wall Street Journal,* copublished by Hearst Magazines (publisher of *Good Housekeeping,* etc.), ran a cover story near the end of 1994

---

*You actually have less, because of taxes on the interest.

about the riskiest mutual funds for investors. The point of the article was to show that "risky" was not necessarily a synonym for "terrible."

In fact, some of these funds performed very well indeed: The AIM Constellation Fund, which invests in smaller companies, grew 17 percent a year over a five-year period. The fund's net asset value, or daily selling price, just happened to bounce around a great deal on its way to that nice return, though, so if a nervous investor happened to be watching the price on a daily basis, he or she probably would have felt increasingly at risk.

Risk Versus Reward

In investing, risk must always be weighed against reward. (It should also be weighed against how much of your total account is involved in a particular fund.)

For example, investing in the stocks of small, highly innovative companies is risky because of many factors. Many of them have not yet produced a product—investing in them is an act of faith. The company might discover a drug to cure cancer or develop a more powerful computer chip. It might be acquired by a richer, more powerful company or enter into a lucrative agreement to supply parts to a popular product. Being there when good news happens is the *reward* for investing in this stock. Unfortunately, promise is not always fulfilled—and that's where the *risk* takes over.

For example, somebody might beat the company to market with a similar (but less expensive) breakthrough, or it might run out of money before hitting pay dirt, or a regulatory agency may not approve its new drug. On the other hand, if the company is successful, the value of an investment in the company's stock could double, triple, or quadruple overnight.

Is it worth taking the chance you'll lose part of your money for the chance to triple it? It depends on the company, the product they're working on, the competition, and so on. The best mutual fund managers investigate all these factors before jumping in—so you don't have to.

Sleepless Nights?

There are other things to consider as well, particularly a fund's style of investing. As an investor instead of a saver, you have to decide what level of risk is right for you. If you are as jumpy as a cat on a hot tin roof, you probably don't want to invest in the most highly speculative funds, because you would like to sleep at night. Of course, you could invest just 10 percent of your account in something like this—enough to take some advantage of the opportunity, but not enough to make you twitch.

> You will find that "risk" isn't necessarily a bad thing unless you don't acknowledge you can't deal with it. But if you're an average robust person, risk can be a good thing.

Taking risks can mean the difference, for example, between a very comfortable retirement and a difficult one.

(See "What's Your Risk Quotient?" page 90, to get an indication of how strong/weak your "heart" probably is.)

The Wages of Volatility

Here's another, related word that investors (particularly new ones) find pretty terrifying: volatility.

What's volatility? There's an old French movie, *The Wages of Fear,* in which a group of down-and-out men are promised outrageous fees for driving truckloads of nitroglycerine across the mountains. Why did these losers rate top dollars for the trip? Because the nitroglycerine was so volatile that it could blow up at any bump in the road. (P.S. It did, and most of the men were blown to smithereens.)

In investing, volatility is the ups and downs of the stock market that, when made into a graph, look like a roller coaster.

> Are you putting your money into the stock market for a six-month or one-year period, ready to pull out if things don't look so good? Volatility is the bump in the road that could help "blow up" your investment.

The volatility of the markets in stocks and bonds is one of the major reasons that you have to know about and take advantage of **asset allocation** (splitting up your investments among stocks, bonds, and cash) and **diversification** (splitting up your contributions among aggressive and index stock funds, short-term bond funds, etc.), to be discussed fully in Chapter 7.

Going to Extremes: Risks You May Not Think About

In the quiz that started this chapter, I gave you pairs of extremes in order to show you that, in most cases, extreme positions won't do well for you. Here's a closer look at why.

Too conservative versus too aggressive

Unshrinkable? I already talked a bit about the drawbacks of choosing what looks like a traditionally conservative investment, for example, a bank savings account. The advantage of putting all your money in this kind of asset is that you know exactly where it is and you can get it anytime you want (particularly if you have an ATM card). Your principal doesn't shrink unless you make a withdrawal, while you accrue interest every month that won't make you rich but does increase your balance. Again, the disadvantage is that you may not outrun inflation.

So, stay away from the conservative, right? Remember 1994? The economy was moving along nicely and corporate profits were up, but the Federal Reserve kept raising interest rates (and threatened more). The stock market did poorly; bonds did, too. While there were industries and individual stocks that were pockets of good news, they were mostly very small. Even some of the most prestigious stock funds were producing losses by the third quarter of '94, because their style of investing was out of favor or their holdings were in industries investors were nervous about.

So a conservative-looking investment like a GIC fund, paying 5, 6, or 7 percent suddenly seemed like a high flyer. And if you were just starting out in your 401(k), it might have been a good place to be *for a while*. (And I emphasize those last three words.) On the other hand, some market pros look at periods with depressed stock prices for good, solid companies as an opportunity to get bargains that, ideally, will improve in saner times. Prices for basically solid funds may do the same.

Stocks are "it." What about 1993, when the market was performing better? Was that a time to put all your money in stock funds? After all, the statistics show that over the last sixty years or so large company stocks have outrun other investment alternatives over the long term, returning an average of 10 percent, and small company stocks did even better (about 12 percent). Even then, you shouldn't put all your eggs in one aggressive stock fund: There have been more than twenty years during that sixty-year period when large company stocks had losses (twenty-one years for small companies).

Split it up. Where does that leave you, since neither extreme is safe all the time? The concept of risk-to-age should help guide you in *splitting up* your money—to be more aggressive when you're younger and time is on your side and less daring as age increases and you can't wait for the market to emerge from a long-lasting nosedive.

Does this mean you must get more conservative as you approach retirement? Only within limits. Being too conservative (that is, taking most of your money out of stocks) means that your money, which might have to last you fifteen or twenty years, won't grow sufficiently. You always need a growth component in your account, no matter how old you are. Some pros even feel that your portfolio should never have less than 50 percent in stocks, although relying more and more on less risky stock funds.

Too many investments versus too few

Many of you won't have to worry about this, because your 401(k) offers little or no choice. But if you have more—say ten options to choose from—how many of them should you take advantage of?

How much is "too many"? There are some schools of thought that say put 10 percent in each and get yourself a really diversified portfolio. Many pros argue that having ten funds in your account is not too many. Frankly, I disagree.

> Ten funds may not be too many from the point of view of diversifying your investment. It is, in my opinion, too many for the average 401(k) investor to think about and keep track of, especially if you're just starting out in the investment game.

After all, you do have other things in your life besides managing your 401(k), even though there may be nothing more important.

To me, four or five—okay, six, tops—are the maximum that makes sense, but only if they are all worthy components of your portfolio. (If you have some IRAs hanging around from the good old days, you have to keep track of them, too.) After all, by investing in a mutual fund, you are automatically diversifying your investment from day one. While you need to have a variety of funds to diversify investment types and the styles of the people who are running the funds, enough is (sometimes) enough.

On the other hand, a diversified portfolio of funds makes a lot more sense than having everything in a single fund, where, if it goes down, you have no protection. Remember, a single option is no option.

Changing investment options too often
versus never changing at all

Protecting yourself. One of the disadvantages of *daily valuation* and a voice-response system—a feature of an increasing number of 401(k)s—is that it allows you to change investment options too easily. I know the temptation. The market slides for a few days and you say, "Oh, no. I have to protect my investment." So you call up the telephone line and switch everything out of your aggressive growth fund and put it in the savings account. Two days later, things calm down and you transfer everything back—only the gyrations haven't really stopped and you want to transfer it out again.

As mentioned earlier, making changes according to the movement of the markets is called *market timing*. Unless you're a crackerjack investor with nerves of iron, you just can't win at this kind of tactic—and even pros make timing errors.

Plus, you run the risk of hitting the downturns and missing the upturns. Lipper Analytical Services, which studies the performance of the Standard & Poor's stock index over time, shows that if you left all your investments intact between 1974 and 1993, you would have ended up with a 12.8 percent average annual return. This is nearly *twice* what you would have gotten from taking your money in and out and missing the best ten months out of that twenty-year period, which was only about 4 percent of the time.

What about sitting pat with your original investments? This is also dangerous. You need to check on your choices *at least* twice a year, to see how they have performed and whether it's the fund or the market in general that may be causing any *negative returns*—that is, "losses."

Also, if one particular area of your account (for example, your stock fund) has outperformed or underperformed the others, you may need to rethink the percentages of your contributions going into each of the investment options. (See section on "Rebalancing" in Chapter 5.)

The thought of daily valuation makes some plan sponsors crazy. They visualize employees spending all their time on the phone changing investments. Or they don't believe their people have the know-how to use this kind of tool well—and that someday it will blow up in the company's face when investments don't turn out okay.

Research has shown, however, that when 401(k) plans switch to daily valuation and allow more frequent account access, changes in employee accounts actually decrease. This is the result of the increased comfort level of participants who know they *could* make a change if they wanted to.

Contributing too little versus starting too late

You're only twenty-five or thirty and have enough trouble making ends meet or simply think that you have better things to do with your money at this point in your life than save for retirement. You think, "What can $25 per pay period do for me? I'll just catch up when I can afford to save a bigger chunk of cash."

I can only refer you back to the example in Chapter 3, which clearly demonstrates the advantage—the *necessity*—of starting as early as you can.

One thing is absolutely certain: It'll cost you a fortune to play "catch-up" if you start too late—but even small amounts can grow enormously if you start early and don't invest too conservatively. That's why this is the exception to the rule of extremes.

Not joining at all versus planning to spend savings prematurely

This is where my own prejudices show through: I believe that the worst thing you can do is pass up your plan, because not only does it offer too many advantages, but you're also going to need it. On the other hand, spending your money prematurely runs a pretty close second.

Look at it this way:

- **Don't join your plan** at all and you run the risk of being left with nothing but Social Security to fund your retirement, which is not much. Unless you're such an unusual American that you can save heavily despite the temptations in front of you, you probably won't end up with a sufficient nest egg. (In any event, you probably could not do as well as through your 401(k).)
- **Spend your money prematurely** and you could end up in exactly the same boat. (Of course, you at least could have a few fond memories or a home to retire in.) If you only borrowed from your plan and didn't liquidate it in changing jobs, etc., you will have to repay the loan.

So I guess that not joining *might be* worse in some few cases. The essential truth is that neither of these is a good option, as should be clear by now.

What You Should Have Learned from This Chapter

1. At an inflation rate of 4 percent, a loaf of bread will increase in cost by almost 50 percent in ten years. That might not seem like much—if your income is going up by 50 percent, too.

2. Guaranteed investment contracts (GICs) may look appealing when the stock market is as wobbly as it was in 1994. But for long-term goals—and retirement planning falls into that category—it won't keep your account growing as fast as it could.

3. *Risk* is not a dirty word—not when it's weighed against the possibility of reward. Some great-performing mutual funds are considered high risk—because they can have many sudden ups and downs on the way to their high return on your investment.

4. Being at the extreme on any issue increases your risks as an investor, whether being too conservative or too aggressive or having your investments divided among too few funds or too many.

5. If you can only start out with small contributions, such as $25 a week when you're twenty-five, should you wait and save more later on in your life when you can afford it? NO! See the example in Chapter 3 for proof that starting early really pays off.

Think About This. . .

What's Your Risk Quotient?

How do you stay ahead of inflation over the long run? Most financial advisers recommend diversifying your portfolio—and leaning on stocks to help punch up the growth of your retirement savings.

But how much of your account should you devote to stocks? It depends on lots of things—starting with how much risk you can take. So you'd better figure out how much risk you can actually take before you choose that superaggressive investment option that you think offers the promise of a future on Easy Street.

Are you conservative or bold? It's not necessarily so easy to figure it out. There are, however, some clear signs. Be as honest as you can about your answers to the following questions, because you're the only one being fooled if you fudge. Everyone's different and it's no reflection on your intelligence if you decide that a more reserved approach is right for you.

1. Time frame. How many years do you have to put together your nest egg?
(a) at least 10   (b) at least 20   (c) at least 30

2. Investment decisions. As a 401(k) participant, you're going to have to make investment decisions. How do you feel about doing this on your own?
(a) I would never do it
(b) I could do it with some effort
(c) I'm confident about doing it

3. Past success. If you've ever invested before, what has your experience been like? (If you haven't invested, you might want to rate yourself on choosing a brand of car or getting a great deal on buying a house or apartment.)
(a) terrible   (b) better than average   (c) great

4. Luck. Do you believe in luck? Have most good things happened to you because of it? Or do you make your own "luck"? Would you say that luck is really
(a) "somebody up there likes me"
(b) opportunities you took
(c) good planning

5. Hold or fold? Even if you've never "played the market," think about this one: You've bought a stock and within months it doubles in price. Would you sell it? Cash in your original investment and hold on to the rest? Buy more?
(a) sell it   (b) sell half   (c) buy more

6. Take the money. What would the potential profit have to be for you to invest 10 or 15 percent of your current savings in a venture that has an excellent chance of success over the next year?
(a) 1000%—and I still wouldn't do it
(b) 50%
(c) 10%

7. Place your bets. If your friend won a free weekend in Las Vegas for two, would you be raring to get to the craps table or slot machines? Have you already spent over $100 at a casino or the track? Do you get together with the boys/girls for poker or bet on your golf game for more than penny-ante stakes?
How often?
(a) I'd rather die
(b) a few times in my life
(c) several times a year

8. Money decisions. When you have to make an important money decision, do you mull it over and over until it goes away? Talk it over with your spouse and do it? Ask your accountant to do it for you? Figure it out for yourself?
(a) close your eyes, hope it will go away, and then make a
     last-minute guess
(b) go to a professional
(c) make a measured decision, with some consideration of
     what others have to say

What your answers say:

While this quiz is not scientific, your answers to the questions say something about your investing tendencies.

1. Did you choose a time frame until the day you retire—or until the end of the fifteen to twenty years you could spend in retirement? If you chose the latter, you probably have a better idea of just how much money you're going to need. That's good. Time, as mentioned earlier, is the best friend of an investor—and the longer you have, the more aggressive you can afford to be.

2. Clearly, making investment decisions takes a degree of confidence. The more you have, the more comfortable you're likely to be with an aggressive approach. If you answered, "I would never do it," I say, "Yes, you will—and might even learn to like it by the time you've finished reading this book."

3. The more successful you've been, the more likely you are to take a chance again. On the other hand, if you've never made a dime, you're apt to be very cautious.

4. The more you believe that you make your own luck, the more likely you are to take a chance on it. On the other hand, if you think that luck is something you either have or don't, you are likely to be extremely careful.

5. The more likely you are to hold on to your investment and even add to it, the happier you'll be with a more aggressive approach to investing. If all you think about is preserving your principal, you should take the more conservative route.

6. If you chose the first option, at least you're honest about how conservative you are. Fifty percent is a darned good return for a pretty safe bet; it's what you can get through company matching even if your account isn't earning interest. If you said 10 percent, it shows you're aggressive enough to take a risk even for a modest return. Ten percent is the annual return the stock market has historically paid long-term investors. Stocks are considered an aggressive investment because of the market's year-to-year volatility.

7. The more often you have taken a chance, the more you'll be able to live with a more aggressive portfolio. On the other hand, if betting terrifies you, you probably should look for the conservative way out in investing.

8. I guess I don't have to tell you that if you "close your eyes, hope it will go away, and then make a last-minute guess," you are not an aggressive investor in the making. However, you do, at the least, have to be comfortable with making the decisions on your own or in conjunction with your spouse. Of course, consulting a professional whose opinion *on investing* you respect makes sense—but then you are relying on someone else to determine how aggressive you want to be. In the end, you're the one who is going to have to live with the investing decision.

Matching your answers to a portfolio:

• If your answers were mostly "a," your view of investing is pretty "Conservative" and you probably don't need the aggravation of being too stock-oriented in your investing. This means you're willing to trade a relatively low return on your money to avoid the ups and downs of more active kinds of investing.

• If your answers were mostly "b," you're pretty "Average"—not ready for the rocking chair, but neither are you going to bet everything on something hot and exciting. This means you're willing to take *some* chances with your investing in order to achieve a better return on your contributions—but only *some*.

• If your answers were mostly "c," you seem to be an "Aggressive" type and you're probably willing to take higher-than-average risks. This means that in order to maximize returns, you're willing to take the long view and invest in more volatile options, such as international or small company stock funds.

For some help in matching your risk quotient to an investment portfolio, see the models in Chapter 8, which are divided into "Conservative," "Average," and "Aggressive" categories.

7

Allocating Your Assets

This chapter deals with asset allocation—deciding how to divide up your 401(k) contributions among stock, bond, and cash-equivalent options.
Before we proceed, here are some things to think about.

DO YOU KNOW . . . ?

1. Which of the following is more important to the final size of your 401(k) account?
    (a) your asset allocation
    (b) the specific stock fund you choose
    (c) the net asset value of the fund on the day you
        bought it
2. If you can get information on asset allocation from mutual fund companies where you're not an investor?
    (a) only if you have a friend working there
    (b) yes, most of the time it's free, if you call an
        800-number
    (c) never in a million years
3. Whether to put most of your money in stocks?
    (a) yes, if you're young and have time to wait out
        market fluctuations
    (b) yes, if you don't care what happens to your
        money
    (c) no, it's a sure way to lose everything

ANSWERS:

1. (a) Asset allocation, according to the experts, can account for 80 percent or more of the total return of your 401(k).
2. (b) Absolutely. Most information from mutual funds is free, whether or not you're a current investor.
3. (a) The longer your time frame, the more risk you should be able to tolerate in your portfolio.

There's a series of radio commercials for a major bank's retirement services that features fictitious investors talking about their questionable investment strategies: One puts "20 percent in domestic stocks, 20 percent in foreign stocks—and 60 percent in my top drawer." Another says she puts "50 percent in stocks and 50 percent in bonds. Why? I have no idea."

They make for funny commercials. Unfortunately, many inexperienced 401(k) participants make their investment choices this way. Even the famous still fall into this trap:

> When Katie Couric did a 401(k) segment on *The Today Show* early in 1995, she admitted that when it comes to choosing the funds for her own 401(k), she guesses.

So, how do you put together a sensible portfolio from the investment options offered by your plan? There are two steps; this chapter covers the first of them: asset allocation. (Chapter 8 covers the other step: making an informed choice from your specific investment options.)

Asset Allocation—Dividing Your Contributions by Type

By this point in the book, I hope that you have a better idea of your feelings about being an investor. The risk test that preceded this chapter should have given you an indication as to whether you have the soul of an aggressive investor, a conservative investor, or are somewhere in between.

Now, what do you do with this information?

Before you take a hard look at your plan's individual options and try to figure out which of them suit your needs, think back for a moment to Chapter 4, which gave some advice on preparing for the enrollment meeting. You read about setting goals that fit your needs; hopefully you have done this.

Now, with (a) your risk tolerance and (b) your goals in mind, let's move on to determine what combination of general investment categories will get you where you want to go: Welcome to the wonderful world of Asset Allocation.

Here, as an informed 401(k) participant, you must decide how you want to divide up your contributions among different types of investments:

Should you put it all in stock?
Split it between stocks and bonds?
How much should go into cash-type investments?

Your Most Important Move

Of all the factors you must consider in choosing your investment options, **asset allocation**—how much of your total contribution you want to invest in stocks versus bonds versus cash equivalents—is the most important. Each asset class is very different from the others and has its own set of pros and cons.

> Why do you need to know about asset allocation? Because it's even more important than the specific investment options you choose; 80 percent or more of your eventual return could depend on it.

A Diversified Portfolio

Traditionally, a diversified long-term investment portfolio would contain a mix of:

- **stocks for growth, because they can increase dramatically in price.** In general, *stocks* are considered the riskiest investments, but also the ones most capable of providing the best long-term returns for your account. (That's why your portfolio should never abandon stock funds, no matter what your age.)
- **bonds for regular income and less risk.** As a class of investment, *bonds* are considered to be less risky, although they have risks of their own. For example, when interest rates are going up—as they did in 1994—corporate bonds and even longerterm U.S. Treasuries can take a dramatic fall in value. There are also bond funds that are risky by nature: If you see a fund called "high yield" or "high return," the high rates are in return for the risk of investing in companies that have less-than-perfect financial standing.
- **cash equivalents for their liquidity—so you can get your hands on them easily.** The least risky investments are *cash* equivalents and U.S. short-term Treasury bills—except if you consider their performance in relation to inflation. Rely on these too heavily and you may preserve your original investment, but not add much to it after taking inflation into account.

As your age increases, the mix of these elements should shift, with more *regular income* and more *liquidity* gradually replacing some *growth* as you approach the age of retirement.

> While having a mixture of investments doesn't always shelter you from the uncertainties of investing—in 1994, for example, stocks *and* bonds took a dive—historically, this has been shown to make sense.

Does It **Really** Make a Difference?

According to data from Ibbotson Associates, a Chicago research firm that follows such things, in the sixty-eight-year period from

1925 to 1993, large and small company stocks were the big winners for investors:

Small company stock	12.36%
Large company stock	10.33%

And if you consider that the average inflation was just 3.13 percent, an investor during that period would have come out way ahead of the game. Going by these figures through 1993, one dollar invested in large company stock back in 1925 had grown to over $800; in small companies, $2,757.

That's pretty good investing, don't you think? And judging from these numbers, you wouldn't think that there was any risk at all in stock investing. Right?

Things That Go Bump

Dream on. Let's look at those numbers again, this time with the range of stock return during those sixty-eight years.

Small company stock	12.36%	highest return 142.9% in '33; lowest −58% in '37
Large company stock	10.33%	highest return 54% in '33; lowest −43.3% in '31

During that same period, inflation ran quite a gamut as well:

Inflation	3.13%	highest 18.2% in '46; lowest −10.3% in '32

In the past seven decades, according to Ibbotson, there were twenty-one years when stocks of small companies (worth under $1 billion today) posted negative average returns and twenty years when stocks of large companies (worth over $5 billion today) had negative returns. During that period, the records show that stocks lost money in two out of every seven years; however, over the last two decades, they lost money only in 1977, 1981, and 1990.

In short, you might place your faith in the returns of stock over the long term, but you could also lose your shirt if you *aren't thinking* long term.

How did bonds do during this same period?

Long-term corporates returned $40 for $1 invested. Government bonds, in comparison, grew to about $28, Treasury bills to just under $12—slightly better than inflation. But long-term governments had eighteen down years and intermediate-term bonds had six down years—though they still beat inflation. Even the thirty-year Treasury bill once had a negative return—though it still managed to squeak past the inflation level.

Diversification is important in assembling a portfolio because the securities markets are just too volatile to put too much faith in one kind of investment. Dividing your contributions lowers that risk.

What the Pros Don't Know

If the responsibility of putting this all together into a portfolio looms large in front of you, well, it should—because allocating assets is hard even for the professionals. That's why there are often articles in *The Wall Street Journal* or *Barron's* or *The New York Times,* for example, showing how the top investment strategists at the major brokerage houses differ substantially on *what* should be invested *where* at a given time. Out of thirteen experts polled by the *Journal* at the end of January 1995, for example, no two agreed totally on what should be invested where: they ranged from 40 percent to 65 percent in stocks, from 0 percent to 40 percent in cash, from 5 percent to 50 percent in bonds.

Talk about a difference of opinion! On the other hand, a number of these pros using totally different approaches manage to come out ahead of the game—showing, once again, that there's more than one way to win at investing.

Dividing the Pie

How do you decide what percentages of stocks, bonds, and cash belong in your portfolio according to your tolerance for risk?

You don't have to make your decisions all alone.

If you are in a company-directed plan, you don't have to worry about it. Plans with few options are sure to include a balanced fund, which helps allocate assets for you. If you are in a plan with more choices, most providers will give you some kind of tool to help you determine the kinds of investments to choose for your account, at least the first time around.

For example, many companies provide a wheel that calculates how much you will end up with at various savings levels at various rates of return, and then give you an accompanying chart that shows you what you need to achieve those rates. Here are the kind of things these calculators can show you:

- If you save $100 a month starting at age thirty and invest conservatively, earning a 4 percent annual return, you will end up with a little more than $90,000 in your account at sixty-five.
- If you are able to earn a return of 6 percent, your total will rise to over $143,000; at 8 percent, you could end up with over $230,000.
- But if you invest aggressively, and are able to raise your return to 10 percent, you will end up with over $380,000.

Double your contributions and these number double—so you can see why it's important to contribute as much as you can to your account!

Many companies offer a similar tool on disk for those who aren't put off by technology; these are great not only for seeing how your account can grow, but for comparing it to the annual amount you'd like to have for retirement. An increasing number of companies have begun to provide counselors to do these calculations for you in person, to encourage you to maximize the level of your contributions to the plan.

You can gather additional information on asset allocation on your own from the big mutual fund companies like Vanguard, Dreyfus, Fidelity, T. Rowe Price, or Scudder, even if you don't happen to be in a plan that features their funds.

Fidelity has "A Common Sense Guide to Planning for Retirement," which talks about various retirement-related issues, including asset allocation, and includes a work sheet that will show you the various combinations of funds that you should think about having at the various stages of your retirement-planning life. Vanguard has its "Investment Planner." Scudder has an appealing series of booklets called "The Scudder Investor Series," including one on retirement. Dreyfus has its "Personal Retirement Planner." All of these are in plain language.

Some of these brochures are free only to the company's fundholders, but none is more than a few dollars (except for some that are on disk). When you call for any of these, you'll get various degrees of "sell" to send you information about specific funds; take whatever they offer—you never know what might be useful.

Having looked over these brochures and many other explanations of how to allocate assets, I can honestly say that their messages do not differ from one another. None contain any stunning revelations. What they *can* do is to help you become better accustomed to dealing with financial information.

Basically, they all tell you that it's smart to be more aggressive and invest higher percentages of your contributions in stocks when you're younger, because over the long term, say twenty years or more, the stock market has consistently proven to provide the best return for your money. Progressively, you should become less aggressive as you approach retirement.

Growth Potential

Since one of the great benefits of the 401(k) is its ability to grow faster than other kinds of savings, you should, by all means, take advantage of it as soon as you can.

This means, according to the experts, not only starting as

early as possible but also saving the maximum amount. It also means that when you are between the ages of twenty-five and, say, your mid-forties, your 401(k) portfolio should have a healthy percentage of stock funds. How much is "healthy"?

> Here's one trick for determining how much of your pot should be in stocks: Subtract your age from 100; the remainder is the percentage of stock funds you should have in your portfolio.

Of course, this is a little too simplistic to work for everybody. Some experts say that, depending how big a swashbuckler you are, your holdings in stock funds could run 10 to 15 percent more than 100 minus your age; a conservative investor, however, may be comfortable with 10 to 15 percent less.

Thus, at twenty-five, your portfolio might be divided something like the pie chart in the center, although you might find yourself better suited to the charts on the left or right. It all depends on your willingness to increase risk for the possibility of higher returns:

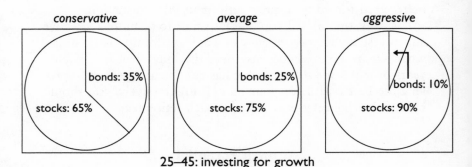

conservative

bonds: 35%

stocks: 65%

average

bonds: 25%

stocks: 75%

aggressive

bonds: 10%

stocks: 90%

25–45: investing for growth

After the age of forty-five or so, the experts say, it's time to start slowing down (although not dramatically), with less in stocks, despite their capacity for growth, and more in bonds, which can bring you more interest income.

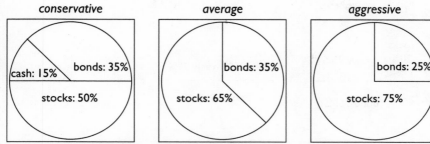

45–60: slowly starting the shift from growth

By the time you reach sixty, you may even be thinking about early retirement. The stability of your nest egg should be increasingly critical, although you still need to think about increasing the value of your portfolio through stocks.

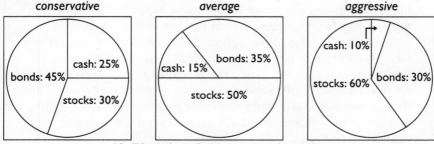

60–70: shifting further toward stability

By seventy, most people will be well into the joys of retirement and concerned that money be there as they need it. Professionals advise shifting the weight of your asset mixture toward regular income and cash—whether you have left your money in your 401(k) or transferred it into an IRA or some other sheltered investment vehicle. Still, since there's an increasingly good chance that you'll be around in your eighties, you'll need stock funds to retain an element of growth.

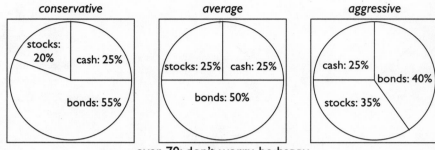

over 70: don't worry, be happy

A Bolder Approach?

That, as I said, has been the traditional way of looking at as-set allocation. Today, with life being longer and more expensive, and with other possible sources of income being less secure, many investment experts are advising a much bolder approach to investing for retirement—even for conservative types.

Some say an aggressive approach is called for when retire-ment is as little as ten to fifteen years away. These experts be-lieve that even when you are as close as five years from retirement, you'll still need the growth potential of stocks (al-though not necessarily with the most aggressive of stock funds) to beef up the return that you'll need to keep you going to, say, age eighty or more.

> There are professionals who say that even if you have as little as seven years until you need your money, then two-thirds should be in stock funds of one sort or another. Long-term bonds? Forget them. Put the rest in short-term investments.

These advisers believe there's not much advantage to invest-ing in bonds, and that if you have enough time to weather the ups and downs of the bond market, then you have enough time to invest in stocks, which are more likely to give a higher return.

On the other hand, the bond market in the eighties and nineties has been generally higher than in any period in history, with average returns of over 12 percent for both long-term corporates and governments and slightly less for intermediate governments.

Jeremy J. Siegel, a professor of finance at the University of Pennsylvania's prestigious Wharton School of Finance, however, is one of those with a high opinion of stock performance. His research shows that even though the stock market is more volatile than the bond market year by year, stocks have done better than bonds over every thirty-year period since 1871.

This is great news, particularly if you're just starting out in retirement saving and your company is offering you good stock funds among its investment options.

What You Should Have Learned from This Chapter

1. Most of the time, asset allocation is even more important than the individual funds you choose in determining the success of your portfolio.
2. Free material available from the large mutual fund companies can help deal with concepts like asset allocation.
3. The experts disagree about the part that bonds should play in asset allocation. But one thing is clear: Stocks provide the best growth prospects.

8

Turning Investment Options into a Portfolio

This chapter is designed to help you look at your plan's invest-ment options and figure out which ones to select, according to the asset allocation you chose in the previous chapter.

Before we go on, here are a couple of questions to get you started:

DO YOU KNOW . . . ?

1. What "high yield" means when referring to a bond fund?
   (a) It's the best investment available
   (b) It's one of the riskiest types of bond fund you can find
   (c) It pays off only when the market is high
2. Why do some plans now have twenty investment op-tions?
   (a) because there are so many mutual funds available
   (b) because the Department of Labor is encourag-ing it
   (c) because the stock market reached a new high

ANSWERS:

1. (b) The bonds in this fund pay a "high yield" because the com-pany issuing them has a lower credit rating, and must pay a higher interest rate in order to attract investors.

2. (b) The Department of Labor provides certain protection to companies offering 401(k)s from future lawsuits if participants are offered increased control over their accounts, including more investment options.

Your decision making doesn't end, of course, with properly allocating your assets. You still have to choose among your investment options. Before you can do that logically, you have to spread them out in front of you, so you can compare them ccording to their levels of risk and record of performance.

Why? Say you decide to take a fairly aggressive approach to your portfolio and put 75 percent of your contributions in stock and 25 percent in bonds. You take a look at your plan and . . . there are four stock funds to choose from:

- an S&P 500 Index fund
- a blue-chip stock fund
- an aggressive growth fund
- an international stock fund

and then there are four bond funds:

- an intermediate government bond fund
- a high-yield bond fund
- a long-term corporate bond fund
- an international bond fund

plus:

- a balanced fund
- a GIC fund
- a lifestyle fund or asset allocation fund
- a savings account

While your investment options will fall into four very broad categories—stock funds, bond funds, balanced/asset allocation/lifestyle funds, and cash-equivalent funds—there are many subcategories within each of these. For example, you can buy:

- *stock funds* that invest in big companies, small companies, companies that are unjustifiably out of favor with the stock market right now, companies in a single industry, companies in a single country or region, and so on.
- *bond funds* that offer you higher interest in return for their riskier nature, or ones that are reasonably stable but provide lower return, or even ones with holdings that have done almost as well as stocks.

Which ones should you pick? Where do all these choices fall as you put together a conservative versus average versus aggressive portfolio—or try to temper the risk you take in any of these investment styles? It all depends on the individual funds offered to you, and how willing you are to take a bigger risk in exchange for the opportunity of greater return someday.

To start, each type of fund will fall into one of three categories:

stock funds	bond funds	cash funds
aggressive growth growth conservative growth	aggressive income income conservative income	GICs savings account money market

Next, each fund will fall into a type relating to its investment approach.

First, the kinds of stock funds that are generally the riskiest funds, but also those that could give you the greatest return in the long term.

aggressive growth	growth	conservative growth
area, country, or emerging markets funds (Latin America, Asia) sector or specialty funds aggressive growth	blue-chip value international stock global stock small-cap stock mid-cap stock growth company	equity income equity index growth and income

Next down on the risk spectrum, the bond funds, which are generally less risky than those with stocks:

aggressive income	income	conservative income
high yield/high income international bond	global bond Ginnie Mae (GNMA) U.S. Treasury Long-Term corporate bond	U.S. Treasury Intermediate short-term bond short-term global bond

Combining aspects of stock and bond funds are the all-in-one, or combination, funds that have a growth component as well as an income component. These may include funds that are called "balanced funds," "lifestyle funds," "life-stage funds," "life-cycle funds," and "asset allocation funds." These may be labeled "lifestyle—income," "asset allocation—growth," or even "life-cycle—aggressive growth"; they are usually less risky than any of the others in their category, but they are still for long-term investors:

all-in-one or combination
balanced lifestyle/life cycle asset allocation

At the bottom of the risk spectrum (when not considering inflation) are the cash funds:

cash
stable income/GICs savings account money market

The names of the funds you find in your plan, however, will not always tell you clearly which category they fall into.

> The names of mutual funds may be downright confusing. That's because there isn't any book of rules that says, "If a fund buys such-and-such kinds of securities, it is called a so-and-so fund."

That's how the 20th Century Value, T. Rowe Price Blue Chip Growth, and Fidelity Equity-Income funds are all classified as growth-and-income funds in *The Individual Investor's Guide to Low-Load Mutual Funds,* which is published by the American Association of Individual Investors. And Fidelity's Equity-Income and Growth & Income funds—for example, with different managers and different holdings—are often categorized as having identical investment goals when publications do their performance roundups (although not by Fidelity).

The moral of this story: Look through your plan material for a chart that shows how each of your investment options fits into the risk/return spectrum. It is probably your best guide to comparing the relative risks of the plan's funds.

Choosing Investment Options Is Easier than You Think

Now you really have to make some choices, particularly if your plan has a broad range of funds. The good news is, I guess, the choices are not all yours, because you can choose only from the menu of investment options in front of you. So you don't have to wade through the pros and cons of five thousand mutual funds plus all the other types of investments that 401(k)s offer.

On the other hand, more and more plans are suddenly offering a wider variety of options. In 1995, for example, General Motors went from offering five options, which used to be considered a pretty decent selection, to forty-three options—an absolutely terrifying prospect for many 401(k) participants.

Why did this big change happen? After all, according to a study by Bryan Pendleton Swats & McAllister in Nashville, quoted in *Money,* plan participation drops dramatically when more than a dozen options are offered.

The main reason is that Big Brother is watching your company: At the start of 1994, the United States Department of Labor put its ERISA provision 404(c) into effect. Basically, this gives your company certain protection from future lawsuits by unhappy plan participants—that is, those whose investments haven't turned out as succesfully as they would have liked when it comes time to retire—if they have given participants certain things.

These include:

- adequate education about basic investment concepts
- control of your account in the form of the ability to change your allocations and investment choices
- an adequate number of investment options—usually at least three.

Compliance with this provision is not mandatory. But many plans decide that it is a good safety net for themselves and go far beyond the call of duty. They sign on to offer their people a new menu of investment choices that far exceeds the requirements suggested by the Labor Department.

> Increasing the number of options is a two-edged sword. Yes, we have more investment options to choose from—but it's also more difficult to figure out which options are the best for our purposes.

The Inside Scoop

Part of being an informed investor means getting as much information as you can about your plan's specific investments before making these decisions. What do you do when you feel you need more information about your options before you can make a decision? This is a problem not always easy to solve.

Any plan will offer you a one-page (or less) summary of each investment option's objectives or a newsletter that lays out, side by side, the objectives of all the choices you can make. Getting more is often difficult, if not impossible.

> Dig as hard as you can for more fund information, though; when in doubt, ask your benefits office to ask your plan's investment manager for anything more that may be useful.

While mutual funds aren't the only kind of investment available in a 401(k), they usually are the best in providing information about themselves. Why? Because when you buy mutual funds as a plan participant, you are entitled to get the same information that any individual investor would get. This means that the SEC is watching to see what funds are saying about themselves—and slapping them on the wrist if they don't like what they see.

More Reading Material

The prospectus. The best piece of information available on any mutual fund—and also the worst—is the prospectus. This booklet presents a picture of a fund without a sales pitch or glossy pictures to distract you from the basic data about it.

Printed on plain paper, it goes into the nitty-gritty of the kinds of investments it makes, how well the fund has done, and how its performance compares to other funds of its type as well as to one of the major performance indices. (This might be the S&P 500 for large U.S. stocks or the Morgan Stanley index of international stocks in Europe, Australasia, and the Far East.)

It will also tell you about the risks involved in investing in this particular fund. If your plan offers standard mutual funds, the prospectus should tell you the fund's *standard deviation.* This

number can be helpful in understanding how risky the fund is—
and it's one time you probably don't want to be a "10," because
the higher the standard deviation number, the greater the fund's
potential for volatility. Of course, a fund can have a high standard deviation and still produce an excellent return—but you
might have to live through lots of ups and downs to get there.

> The big problem with the prospectus is that it is designed to
> satisfy the SEC, not you and me. The result is that it can be dif-
> ficult to understand, with overly complex language and excess
> information that you don't really care about.

This is particularly true because funds don't print separate
prospectuses for 401(k) participants and individual investors;
the result is that you get information about buying and selling
and other activities that have nothing to do with your plan.

Risk revealed? The SEC is always trying to get funds to provide
more information to investors in a way that they can understand. In 1994, the SEC recommended that mutual fund sponsors be required to provide shareholders with a better idea of
the risk involved in buying a particular fund. While this is not
related to inflation risk, it is tied to the other kinds of risk discussed earlier:

- How much does a change in interest rates affect a portfolio
  of fixed-income securities (that is, bonds)?
- How much has a fund's total return varied, from greatest
  gain to greatest loss, during specific periods of time?
- What is the fund's level of risk relative to that of the overall market?

Will this simplify your life? Perhaps. Will it take the risk out
of investing? Of course not.

Mini-prospectus coming? The SEC has been encouraging mutual fund companies to produce what they call an "off-the-page prospectus." This one-page document would be attached to the regular prospectus to give highlights of major fund features. It is not meant to be a substitute for the full prospectus—the SEC used focus groups to determine that the short version was not enough for investors to base decisions on. This is, however, still in the development stage, with prototypes for stock, bond, and money market funds being produced by eight companies: Vanguard, Fidelity, Scudder, Bank of America, IDS, Capital Research & Management (the American Funds), Dreyfus, and T. Rowe Price. It could be a number of years before these models become standard investment tools in 401(k) kits. (The SEC is also getting after funds to use simpler language in their full prospectuses—but I think we will all be retired before this happens!)

Annual report. Another helpful publication offered by mutual funds is the annual report. Specifically, there is one extremely useful chart: a graph that shows how the value of an initial investment of $10,000 has increased over the lifetime of the fund compared with the increase in a benchmark such as the Standard & Poor's 500 Index over the same period of time.

> You'll see disclaimers that "past performance does not guarantee future results." But you won't find a better indication of the long-term results the fund is capable of providing than the annual report's chart showing performance over time.

What should you look for? If a fund does not perform nearly as well as the index to which it is compared, it should be approached very cautiously—if at all.

The Easier Way

Before I give you a nice, neat rundown of the kinds of funds that you will frequently find in a 401(k) and what each of them offers, I would like to talk about two kinds of funds. They may be of interest to you if you don't have the time, inclination, or interest in really evaluating all your options:

- Balanced/Asset Allocation/Lifestyle funds
- Stock Index funds

The first, which may prove to be justifiably popular, includes many funds that are untested for long-term performance; the second is a less risky way to invest in stocks that can provide as good returns as riskier investments.

Balanced/Asset Allocation/Lifestyle Funds

Whatever names these funds happen to go by, they offer one thing that is undeniably appealing, particularly for first-time investors. They appear to take over the basic work of investing, by constructing a diversified portfolio that, theoretically, you don't have to think about.

Traditionally, multi-asset mutual funds were called balanced funds, since they "balanced" stocks and bonds in a single investment. The idea was to give the money you invest extra protection, because stocks and bonds usually travel in opposite directions. (As I've mentioned, 1994 proved an exception to the rule, as the prices of both stocks and bonds fell.) While these funds could do some shifting of proportions according to market conditions, and hold some of their assets in cash, their basic formula holds stocks to no more than 65 percent of the portfolio. This becomes a distinct disadvantage during a downturn in the bond markets, when a larger proportion of stocks might be in order.

More recently, as *asset allocation* and *lifestyle* have become catchwords, these names—or variations of them—have become parts of fund names—for example, Vanguard Lifestrategy funds, Stagecoach LifePath funds, and Fidelity Asset Manager funds. Theoretically, they are designed to be more flexible than balanced funds in their ability to shift the proportions of stocks, bonds, and cash, according to market conditions: They can lean all the way toward stocks when stocks are in favor and all the way toward bonds when bonds are in favor—or even according to their own feelings about where the market is heading.

Smart Money reported on a couple of asset allocation funds in its April 1995 issue: On January 31, Dean Witter Managed Assets had 100 percent of its assets in cash, while Kidder Peabody Asset Allocation had 98.8 percent in stock.

Are there really any differences among these types of combination funds? Probably.

Longevity. At the moment, most *balanced funds* have an important advantage: longevity. They have been around long enough to have a track record for you to evaluate in black and white, while most of the asset allocation/lifestyle funds were begun within the last two years or so. (There are, of course, some new funds that do very well right from the start; in this case, you have to base your choice on the track record of the manager or mutual fund company offering the fund.)

Style. As far as I can tell, the biggest plus of many asset allocation funds is that they may fit your investment style more closely—for example, by being designed to be income or growth oriented. However, the flexibility of some of these funds gives them the opportunity to take greater risks than you may have bargained for.

Advice. Lifestyle or life-cycle funds are becoming increasingly popular, because they are designed to go about as far as funds can in telling participants how to invest without officially offering "investment advice."

Sometimes they are designed for a specific age group: "If you are twenty-five, this fund may be for you, since it's more aggressive, and you have more time until retirement to ride the ups and downs of the markets." "If you're fifty-five, this fund is worth considering, because it's less aggressive than most, and your retirement is not so far in the future." Other times, they do it according to the date of retirement. "If you're going to retire in 2015, this fund that can help you achieve maximum return."

Some of the people who run education programs for 401(k)s are a little uneasy about lifestyle funds because they allow participants to think they are off the hook and don't have to learn anything at all about investing. My major hesitation about this particular group of funds is that they are designed for the "average" investor of a certain age. If you happen to be more aggressive, they do not always take that into consideration—for example, if you're sixty and hope to live another thirty years, there's no reason not to invest more aggressively. On the other hand, if your risk quotient is average, they can suit you just fine.

Stock Index Funds

The stock index fund (also called "equity index fund") is another simplifier, offering a mix of stocks that approximates one of the major performance indices. Most likely, the index fund in your 401(k) will follow the S&P 500, a standard gauge of U.S. stock performance, geared toward big, well-established companies but representing others as well. (There are bond index funds as well, but not nearly as many.)

Other indices used include the Russell 2000 Index (small companies), the Wilshire 5000 Index (all publicly listed stocks in the U.S.), the Lehman Brothers Aggregate Bond Index (U.S. Treasury and agency securities), the Morgan Stanley International Index mentioned earlier—and there are lots of others. In fact, the Vanguard Group offers more than a dozen different index funds, and some funds have devised their own measurements—for example, the Schwab 1000 Index of America's one thousand largest publicly traded companies.

An index fund is usually considered a less risky option than other kinds of stock funds—yet often outperforms them. (Between 1985 and 1994, for example, only a quarter of stock funds outperformed the S&P 500.)

Index funds offer some benefits of stock investing, but without the likelihood of the kind of high-flying returns that, for example, Fidelity Magellan had in its heyday. The major downside of choosing an index fund is that it is usually geared to a single type of stock. When the S&P 500 is up/down, for example, funds using this measure perform in the same way. There is nothing wrong with this, except that if stocks not in the S&P 500 are the ones to beat during a certain period, you'll miss out. (Small company stocks far outran those of larger companies in the sixties, seventies, and in 1991.)

For the less-experienced investor, this is definitely a lower-risk way than, say, through a growth fund, to become a player in the performance of the stock market. And think about this: When *The Wall Street Journal* challenged top investment pros to beat the returns of the S&P 500 and stocks chosen haphazardly by darts thrown at the stock listings in May '95, the pros beat the dart players handily. They did *not* beat the S&P index.

Funds You May Find in Your Plan

In addition to the combination and index funds just mentioned, here are the most popular kinds of funds that can be found in 401(k)s. Please note that the descriptions discuss the major types of securities that can be found in the funds; in addition, all these funds give their managers leeway to buy a certain percentage of other types of securities.

Stock Funds

Aggressive Growth Funds—Offering Very High Risk and Possible Highest Return

Aggressive stock funds are one kind of fund for people who can tolerate a great deal of risk. This kind of fund usually invests in stocks of small, innovative companies, which have been shown to outperform other kinds of stocks by as much as 2 percent over the long term. As discussed earlier (see Chapter 6), this kind of fund can be highly volatile, going up and down radically in the course of business, even if it eventually shows a great return. If you can't live with this kind of action, look elsewhere, except for modest portions of your account!

Area, regional, or emerging markets funds are usually among the most risky way of investing in the stocks of companies outside the United States. Today, the most popular of these funds are based in Latin America, Asia, and Eastern Europe—all extremely volatile places for investors.

Besides having all the other risks of foreign funds—for example, currency fluctuations—area, regional, or emerging markets funds also bet on the continued calm political and economic climates of the areas in which they invest. These funds can have great years, when they go up 40 percent, 50 percent, or 60 percent—and then plunge that much or more the following year. You probably don't have to worry about finding such funds in your plan, unless your company is one of those with thirty or forty options, because they are considered a bit "far out" for most investors.

Sector or specialty funds can only perform as well as the stocks in the sector they are in. This is one area where timing *is* everything. If gold is up, for example, then a precious metals fund might be appealing; if inflation is down, the time would not be right for this kind of fund.

Among the most popular kinds of funds in recent years are those covering the health-care industry, particularly those with biotech stocks (for example, those responsible for many medical breakthroughs). However, these funds took a beating due to the uncertainty while health-care reform was being debated in Washington, D.C.—and so did their investors.

Company Stock—X, the Unknown

Company stock is in a class by itself. While your company may be in good financial condition and its stock may be a perfectly fine investment, the pros consider this category to be among the riskiest investments for a 401(k). Why? Because you are betting your retirement on the continued health of the company and its stock, and while some bets turn out well, others leave you with nothing but grief.

You may have no choice in holding some of your company's stock in your account because matching contributions are often made this way. But there are actually thirty companies that offer nothing *but* company stock in their plans, according to benefits consultants Hewitt Associates.

Otherwise, the pros usually say not to lean too heavily on this option, unless you know something they don't know, or work for a company that has a great track record, superb financials, and a fabulous future.

(I will also leave out company stock that may be a "given" in dealing with your portfolio. In assembling a diversified portfolio in the coming section, I will deal only with those parts of your portfolio that are under your control—that is, leaving out company stock that is given as matching.)

Growth Funds—Offering High Risk
and Possible High Return

Blue-chip or large-cap funds invest in the stocks of larger well-established companies ("blue-chip stocks") that expect to keep growing at an above-average rate—Coca-Cola, for example, has grown impressively year after year. Dividends may be paid by some of the stocks, but are secondary to the possibility of the stocks' increasing in price.

Mid-cap funds concentrate on midsize companies expected to grow at an above-average rate. Dividends may be paid, but are really coincidental; price increase is the major goal.

Small-cap funds invest most of their assets in small but established companies that are well positioned to increase their price, as opposed to up-and-comers run by risk-takers that might be part of an aggressive stock fund.

Growth company funds combine any of the investments with above-average growth prospects that might find their way into one of the three funds just described. Usually, the companies included in a growth stock fund are well established and have a record that can be evaluated, making them less risky than those in an aggressive growth stock fund.

International/global funds. According to the experts, more than 60 percent of the world's stock opportunities are outside the United States, and they're increasing all the time. A recent ad from Merrill Lynch recommended that 25 percent of a portfolio be invested globally.

If you're a long-term investor—and, 401(k) participants, this means *you*—the returns of foreign investing are believed to outpace U.S. equity returns over the long term.

Over each of the last ten consecutive ten-year periods, international stocks have outperformed their U.S. equivalents, although under-performing the U.S. markets in the nineties. But they are not a sure thing. In addition to all the risks that we have talked about regarding U.S. stocks, foreign stocks may be subject to currency swings (the value of Mexican stock, for example, dropped when the peso was devalued in December 1994).

Records show, however, that if 20 to 30 percent of your portfolio had been in foreign stocks over the last forty years, you'd have done better than with U.S.-only equities. There are two kinds of foreign stock funds you are most likely to find in your 401(k):

- *International stock funds,* which invest in companies outside the United States. There are also stock funds that are international *and* aggressive or international *and* small company, which increases their risk even more.

- *Global/world stock funds,* which can invest in companies that are foreign based *or* in the U.S., although the U.S. portion is usually restricted to a modest percentage.

You would probably be surprised to learn that you may already own international stocks without even knowing it. You might unsuspectingly inherit them through a U.S. fund that has gone overboard in diversifying internationally to increase its return. The result is a fund that is much more aggressive than you thought it was: The Mexican telephone company, Teléfonos de México, was considered a "good buy" and became very popular with mutual funds—until the 1994 devaluation of the peso. Foreign stocks are traded on the New York Stock Exchange as "American Depositary Receipts," as Téléfonos is. You might want to check your own domestic funds' international stakes before buying a piece of the world for yourself in a totally foreign fund.

Value funds buy into basically sound companies that have had decent performance, but have lower stock prices because they have fallen out of favor with investors for what fund managers consider the wrong reasons: For example, they may produce a dull but necessary product or have disappointed Wall Street analysts with lower-than-expected (but still respectable) results.

Conservative Growth Funds—Offering Moderate Risk and Possible Moderate-to-Good Return

Equity-Income funds are more interested in stocks that have a good record of paying dividends than in those with a better-than-average chance of having an impressive increase in price.

Growth & Income funds generally look for well-established companies that have the prospect of increasing in price and pay good dividends. They may have preferred stock (likely to pay higher dividends), as well as common stock (likely to have better growth), along with some bonds. They often do as well as growth funds that have more risk.

Stock/equity index funds (see explanation at the beginning of this section, page 117).

Bond Funds

Aggressive Income—Offering High Risk
and Possible High Return

High-yield/high-income funds invest at least two-thirds of their assets in the corporate bonds of companies that the rating services such as Standard & Poor's or Moody's see as high risk because of their lower credit quality. In return for this risk, the bonds pay a much higher interest rate than you would get from more fiscally sound companies. These funds are considered to be as risky as most stock funds.

International bond funds invest in the higher-grade bonds of companies based outside the United States. Similar to the International Stock funds, they may offer better returns than their U.S. equivalents, but there are political and economic risks that you must be able to accept when you invest in them.

Income—Offering Moderate to Moderately
High Risk and Moderate Return

Ginnie Mae (GNMA) funds seek income by investing mainly in mortgage securities backed by the Government National Mortgage Association, commonly called "Ginnie Mae" in investment circles. They offer a higher-yielding alternative to Treasury-based funds, with equivalent credit quality, but are still sensitive to interest rate changes by the Federal Reserve.

Global bond funds have much in common with Global Stock funds: They invest in companies based in the U.S. as well as those around the world. They are, however, considered a little less volatile than foreign-only bond funds because of the U.S. component of their portfolios.

U.S. Treasury long-term funds are generally more sensitive to changes in interest rates than short-term bonds and are, thus, riskier than their shorter-term "cousins."

Conservative Income—Offering Lower Risk
and Lower Return

Short-term bond funds are considered less risky than long-term funds because short-term bonds aren't as sensitive to interest rate changes. When the Federal Reserve raises interest rates, these don't automatically become less desirable and see their prices plummet.

Short-term global bond funds are similar to the Global Bond funds—except less volatile because of the shorter duration of the bonds the funds hold (although you can still get stung).

U.S. income funds invest in a broad range of government securities, from Treasury bills to federally guaranteed mortgage-backed securities, to give your account a regular flow of cash.

Cash Equivalents—(Usually) Offering the Lowest Risk and Low Return

Government money market funds invest exclusively in U.S. government securities of one sort or another. This is considered more risky—but not much—than some other funds that invest in Treasury bills, because some of the securities are backed by the specific institution that issues them—for instance, Fannie Mae, a "cousin" of Ginnie Mae (see page 123), which stands for the Federal National Mortgage Association.

Taxable money market funds seek current income as well as stability, usually investing in short-term, high-grade securities that are considered the safest available. These might include commercial paper (a kind of IOU issued by corporations) and obligations of financial institutions, U.S. government obligations such as Treasury bills, and CDs of large banks—usually having a maturity date of less than three months.

Money market funds are not precluded from making very risky investments, such as *derivatives*—financial instruments that are supposed to help control the risk of volatile interest and exchange rates, but may cause their own problems.

Money market funds are usually considered a good place to "park" your money while waiting for something better to come along—like an investment that will give you a higher return—or if you're planning to use the money shortly.

Guaranteed Investment Contract (GIC) funds. While not technically "cash equivalents," GIC funds function as such in some plans, offering an interest rate that is an average of all the rates of the contracts it owns. As contracts expire and are replaced, this blended rate will go up or down, depending on the new security's interest. As explained earlier, the health of the issuer is a major risk factor in GIC funds.

People fell in love with these investments in the eighties when many were paying 14 percent or more. The love affair is not over yet, despite lower rates and bad investments that have plagued some GICs. *Marshall Loeb's 1994 Money Guide* estimated that 65 percent of the money in 401(k)-type plans is in GICs, although other estimates have shown a marked decline in GIC assets, particularly where plans provide investing seminars.

Plan providers and sponsors hate GICs despite (or because of) their popularity with participants.

Your option may be called a stable value fund, or guaranteed interest fund, or interest income fund. Whatever its name, the plan will discourage you from investing in it, because the pros don't think this is where your money should be.

There are several reasons for this.

First, it is considered too conservative an option—paying interest that is too low—to make your account grow large enough in the long term to outrace inflation. People who remember the high yields offered by GICs in the eighties may be unaware that current rates are far lower.

Second, the definition and even the safety of GICs is misunderstood by fund-holders. The only thing that is "guaranteed" about a GIC fund is the interest for a particular quarter—there is no guarantee of anything else. And GICs are not insured by the U.S. government.

Third, many investors think that GICs are as safe as cash; in fact, the value of GICs can fall along with the financial strength of the insurance companies or banks that issue them. In the eighties, for example, lots of insurance companies got into trouble because of the quality of the investments in their contracts.

If your retirement is more than ten years away, the GIC fund is far from the best option in your plan—the S&P 500 Index, the standard gauge of stock performance, has outperformed GICs in seven of the past ten years.

One final note: Early in 1995, *The Wall Street Journal* reported that many 401(k)s hold "a great number" of GICs from troubled insurance companies whose yields have declined in value —to a range between 0 and 4.5 percent, versus 6.26 to 8.36 percent from healthy ones—but plan participants aren't being told.

This is particularly problematic for small companies whose plan option holds GICs from a single insurer; in comparison, the fund manager of a larger plan with more to invest can spread employee money among contracts from various issuers, thus minimizing the impact of isolated problems. (This, again, highlights the importance of diversification—don't put all your GICs in one basket.)

Putting the Funds to Work

Now that you know what each of these is, how do you make them work together for you?

As implied before, you can simplify your portfolio by investing in a lifestyle or asset allocation fund, and rely on the reputation and record of the fund managers. You can also rely on stock index funds and corporate or intermediate Treasury bonds and feel you've diversified enough. If your plan happens to offer ten or twenty investment options, you could think about dividing your portfolio equally into ten different funds. The money in your account is yours and you can do whatever you want.

You will find below some suggestions for dividing up your account into a *manageable* number of funds. These are based on conventional wisdom about diversification culled from a variety of expert sources. What do you do if you don't have as many options as mentioned? Less diversification—and a request to your company for more choices might be in order.

> Don't forget: There can be a vast difference in the performance of funds in *any* category. Make sure you know how well a *specific* fund has performed before choosing it. Do not assume that all your plan's investments are of equal quality.

One more warning: While stock funds may differ by their level of risk or the kinds of companies they invest in, *investing in stocks* generally means a higher risk than in bonds or cash equivalents.

Diversifying Your Portfolio

The asset allocation charts in Chapter 7 are the basis of the model portfolios shown below. The charts here feature fund types frequently found in 401(k)s, rather than specific funds, since not every fund is offered in every plan. (For example, you will find an S&P 500 stock index fund as a choice, but not the Vanguard 500 Index Fund.) Matching fund types to your asset allocation is the main point here.

25–45: The Growth Years

Conservative. Of the 65 percent of the portfolio allocated to stocks, most could go into a stock index fund, usually a pretty conservative choice as stock funds go, but one that performs well. Putting 15 percent in a growth fund could add some zip to your return. As for bonds, you might want to divide your contributions between a high-quality corporate bond fund and a short-term fund, as below.

Average. According to the professionals, 75 percent of your portfolio invested in stocks can really punch up your return. You may want to diversify among index, international, and aggressive growth stock funds. With your allocation in bond funds, you might want to be aggressive with part of it and go for high yield, with the rest in a more traditional corporate bond fund.

Aggressive. If you are going all-out with stock funds, you probably want to consider a very heavy concentration in the most aggressive funds, with smaller positions in other stock funds. The remaining 10 percent could go into a traditional bond fund—or into a high-yield fund, for a bolder move.

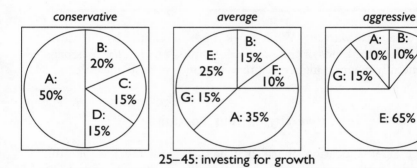

conservative   average   aggressive

25–45: investing for growth

A. S&P 500 stock index
B. long-term corporate bond
C. short-term bond
D. growth company stock

E. aggressive growth stock
F. high yield bond
G. international stock

45–60: Shifting Down a Notch—but Only Just

Conservative. For growth purposes, an S&P 500 stock index fund seems a pretty conservative place to be—following the path set by the general trend of the market. A growth & income fund might give a little edge to it—but not too much. A stable income fund (GIC) will probably be the highest-paying place for cash. Short-term bonds are a low-risk place for income, the intermediate Treasuries moderately more risky.

Average. At this point, decreasing your equity fund holdings by 10 percent might be in order, dividing the remainder among stock funds that range from the fairly conservative (index) to the fairly aggressive (growth). Bond funds might be divided between corporate bonds and, for some higher return, 10 percent in Intermediate Treasury. Cash? It's up to you; you might want to transfer 10 to 15 percent of your aggressive holdings to cash when you hit the sixty milestone.

conservative	average	aggressive
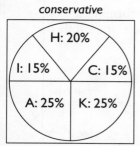	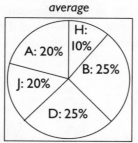	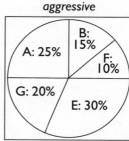

45–60: starting the shift from growth

A. S&P 500 stock index
B. long-term corporate bond
C. short-term bond
D. growth company stock
E. aggressive growth stock
F. high yield bond

G. international stock
H. U.S. Treasury Intermediate bond
I. stable income
J. blue-chip stock
K. growth & income

Aggressive. Still pretty aggressive here, with 75 percent in stock funds, although the 20 percent in an S&P 500 index fund takes a bit of the edge off. Dividing the bond funds between long-term corporate and short-term starts to add some additional income to your portfolio—but still without a real cash component.

60–70: Shifting Down for Retirement

Conservative. Bonds outweigh stocks by three to two; maturities are staggered to boost income while still controlling risk. Cash equivalents: still 25 percent.

Average. Stock funds still could be half your portfolio to provide the growth for what might be another quarter century ahead of you, but shifting from the most volatile. The rest: bonds for income, cash for "capital preservation" and income.

Aggressive. Stock funds remain the largest part of the portfolio, with even a small company component (although geared toward well-established businesses rather than up-and-comers). International stock could beef up your growth; S&P 500 stock index lets you be part of general domestic performance. Long-term corporate bonds add income—and a touch of cash in stable income or short-term bonds for stability.

conservative	average	aggressive
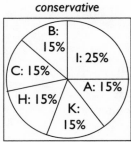	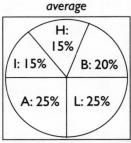	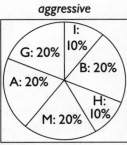

60–70: shifting further toward stability

A. S&P 500 stock index
B. long-term corporate bond
C. short-term bond
G. international stock
H. U.S. Treasury Intermediate bond

I. stable income
K. growth & income
L. value stock
M. mid-cap. stock

Over 70: Retirement Focus

Conservative. A stock index fund gives the possibility of growth with market trends, but otherwise the portfolio is income oriented.

Average. This is income oriented, too, only slightly more weighted with stock funds (including a slightly livelier choice).

Aggressive. About a third of the portfolio remains in stock funds, including a growth component to keep it moving.

A reminder: These portfolios are for reference only. Evaluate the specific investment options in your plan based on their performance records, the state of the economy, and interest rates—and your risk tolerance.

conservative

average

aggressive

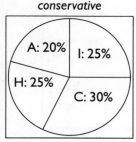
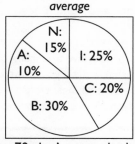
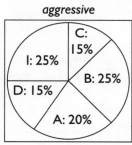

Over 70: don't worry, be happy

A. S&P 500 stock index
B. long-term corporate bond
C. short-term bond
D. growth company stock

H. U.S. Treasury Intermediate bond
I. stable income
N. equity income

What You Should Have Learned from This Chapter

1. Diversification—splitting up your investment among a number of funds—is important because the securities markets are just too volatile to entrust with all your money.

2. In today's economic environment, many investment experts advise a bolder approach to retirement investing than tradition allowed—even when retirement is only ten to fifteen years away.

3. Many plans now offer twenty or more investment options to choose from. More choices, yes, but also more responsibility to figure out which options are the best for our purposes.

. . . And Keep This in Mind

Fasten Your Seat Belt—Dealing with Market Uncertainty

If you haven't noticed, what goes up very often comes down . . . including your stock and bond funds.

So what do you do?

As the title of this section says, "Fasten your seat belt." While your 401(k) may not have an airbag to protect you from the kinds of damage that a jittery market can cause, you certainly don't want to make things worse—and you can. Here are a few *DON'TS* when all you want to do is run for cover.

Don't try to outguess the market.

This is probably a good one to start with because it's the one *nobody* ever listens to, no matter who is giving the advice. But here goes: Moving your money around as you try to outguess the movement of the stock market—whether it is going to drop further or is ready to start climbing again—is a losing proposition.

Why? Because nobody really knows for sure what it's going to do. (And if they do know, do you really think they're going to tell *you* and *me?*) You're going to see and hear too much conflicting information for you to make a decision on what to do: You're just as likely to hear "The Dow is going to lose 40 percent by next year" as "The Dow is going to reach an all-time high within twelve months." The key is to try to act rationally, not emotionally—and remind yourself that you're investing for the long term.

I know that some of you will not be able to remain calm during this kind of situation. I can only tell you what some experts say to do in this kind of situation: If you feel that you have to do *something,* change your future allocations to one of those short-term safe havens (for example, a GIC or money market fund) until things look a little calmer. Others say that you should just leave your account alone, since new contributions will be buying funds at a lower price than in an up market—remember *dollar cost averaging?*

Don't lose your nerve.

People who were nervous about going into the market in the first place find that a downturn is a great excuse to go back into hibernation—that is, putting all their money in a low-interest, low-risk fund option. Don't fall into this trap.

In the long run, you'll only be shooting yourself in the foot if you put your money in a money market or other such conservative investment, because stock investing offers you the only way to outrun inflation over the long term. It may look like the end of the world as the news shouts "DOWN! DOWN! DOWN!" for your investments, but over a longer period of time, it really can be just a blip.

A ten-year study of a thousand equity mutual fund investors by Dalbar Associates, quoted in a brochure from the AIM family of funds, has some interesting insights into the subject of sitting tight. It found that investors who did not sell their mutual funds during periods of market uncertainty did 18 percent better than those who became spooked by turbulence and went in and out of the market.

I know from personal experience that this is a lot easier to say than to do—I've sold depressed mutual funds too soon and seen their prices bounce back. But keeping a calm head really works, and it's easier if you don't look at your funds' performance every single day to see whether or not you're ahead.

Don't lose track of your vision.

In the world of big business today, there are a couple of words that get tossed around quite a bit. Two, in particular, are used interchangeably, although they are, in fact, quite different.

The first is *mission* and the second is *vision*. Of the two, the second is decidedly the more important. Why? Let's look at your mission in terms of this book: "To accumulate enough money for me to have a comfortable/fantastic retirement." That's great—except it hasn't told you how you're going to get there. That's when the vision comes in: "To accumulate enough money for me to have a comfortable/fantastic retirement by taking advantage of my 401(k), which gives me access to three ways to get the most out of my money: investing in stock, compounding, and deferred taxes."

In order to do this, you can't let up when you have a reversal of your plan's performance. Hibernating in a low-risk option may be fine for today, but if becoming a monarch butterfly is your goal, you can't stay in a cocoon forever.

PART IV

Watching Out for Yourself: Rollovers, Retirement, and the Dilemma of Premature Withdrawals

9

Take the Money and Run: What to Do When You Leave Your Job or Retire

This chapter deals with getting your money out of your company's plan with the least pain and the most gain, whether you're retiring or just leaving your job.

Yes, Virginia, you can take it with you!

If you find a new and better job or are job-eliminated or even when you retire, you have to do something with the plan money you've been accumulating.

No matter why you're leaving the company, no matter what your age, you have choices in front of you: Even if you're under 59½, you could, for instance, take a *lump-sum distribution* or *roll over* your money or take a *payout*.

If you thought that any other part of belonging to a 401(k) was complicated, you ain't seen nothin' yet. But hang on. Here is an overview of the basics for getting all the money that's coming to you.

When You Leave Your Job

The vested balance of your 401(k)—everything you've contributed, employer matching that has become yours, plus all account earnings—belongs to you. This means you have some thinking to do about its future when you leave your job.

Taking a Lump-Sum Distribution

Lump sum means just what it says: You get your money in one big lump. If you've ever dreamed about having a pile of cash to do with what you wish, this may be your only chance. On the other hand, it won't be there down the road when you find yourself moaning, "If only I hadn't spent all that 401(k) money in Atlantic City!"

One provider calls its guide to distributions "Taking Your Lumps." It's a cute line that some copywriter toiled over; unfortunately, it's very accurate: If you take this kind of distribution, you *will* take some lumps, in the guise of penalties.

You will have to pay a 10 percent penalty to the IRS if you:

- are under 59½
- left your job without retiring
- decided against saving your 401(k) for later in life
- want to spend the money *now*.

Not painful enough? The IRS requires that your company withhold another 20 percent "just in case" you owe taxes. So you're left with only 70 percent of what you had in your account—unless you owe *more* taxes on April 15. (Count on it and save more money for Uncle Sam.)

Your Rollover Choices

A *rollover* simply means moving your money from one place to another where it can *continue growing tax-deferred*.

A rollover should be your choice when you leave your job for any reason—at least from the point of view of the experts. Let's face it, you're going to need the money. So why not make believe that you don't have the option of using it now and just au-

tomatically stick it someplace where compounding can continue
to do its magic!

> Ideally, you will never actually touch the money in your ac-
> count during the rollover process. It will come right out of
> your current 401(k) and go directly into another account with
> similar tax-deferred benefits until you retire.

But where should you put it? Unless interest rates have
climbed back to 12 percent or 14 percent by the time you read
this—highly unlikely—you probably won't be doing your best
with a short-term solution like a bank CD.

A *new 401(k)*. If your new employer has a 401(k), the company
may permit you to roll over your money directly into its plan,
once it has determined that your old company had a *qualified*
plan. (This means that everything was on the up-and-up according to IRS regulations.)

Whatever you do, don't jump right into it. It may seem like
the easy way out, but not all plans are a great opportunity as a
rollover. You'll need to take the time to see what your new plan
is all about—what kind of performance the investment alternatives have had over time, what kind of opportunities you have
to switch from one option to another, and so on.

**I've seen big plans with few and poorly performing funds, and
little account access. Employer-directed plans give you no say at
all. You might be better off looking for something else to do
with your money.**

That's *not* to say that you should write off the new company's
401(k) completely, even if you do decide to roll over your
money elsewhere. When enrollment time comes around—usually after you've been in your new job a year—join and contribute at least enough to get any matching, even if you don't
like the investment options. Plus, many plans actually improve
with age, with new options and better access being added, especially now that the government is taking a keener interest in
what we are getting out of them. (A rollover to another 401(k)

will also allow you something an IRA does not: loan access in an emergency.)

An IRA. What can be "something better" than a new 401(k) to do with your plan money? Sometimes, putting it directly into a rollover IRA. The key word is *directly:* Don't even think of taking possession of your money for even one day. (See page 142 for more.)

You may already have one or two IRAs from the days when they were a tax benefit for anyone who filed a tax return. A rollover IRA lets you keep the tax-deferred saving benefits of your 401(k), with more investment choices than a 401(k) can offer. In addition, if your rollover is kept separate from any other IRAs you have, you may be able to roll it *back* to another 401(k), if some future job allows it.

With so many funds to consider, how do you start to choose? Cost-wise, you must choose between those charging a load (another name for **commission**) and no-load funds.

For convenience, you might consider the Schwab, Fidelity, or Waterhouse networks. They offer great flexibility in switching among fund families, featuring both load and no-load varieties, although not all funds are represented.

You can also open a mutual fund account at a bank or through a brokerage firm; it will, however, most likely to be more expensive to do so, since you will pay a commission of probably 5.50 percent or more of the amount you're investing. While there are numerous funds that may be worth buying at an additional cost (Putnam Voyager and Oppenheimer Main Street are two that come to mind), many are not. Make sure to check out a fund's current and historic returns—and subtract the load—before making a decision.

So here you are again: Which fund do you choose?

Do you feel that you can't wait one more day to get your money out of your former employer's hands? Then open your rollover with a money market fund wherever you're considering placing your account, so you can easily switch funds later.

This way, you can take control of your money and make a modest return while you figure out what to do for the *long term* (which is what this kind of investment is all about, unless you are very close to retirement). When you've chosen an investment that fits in with the rest of your retirement savings, you can call up the fund's 800-number and make a change.

A little research before you move your account will give you a broader range of choices. *Money, Kiplinger's,* and *Smart Money* spend a good deal of time looking into the performance of various funds and can give you help in narrowing the field, and their comparative charts can help make your work simpler.

Just remember that the choices featured by personal finance magazines aren't foolproof, or there would be lots more millionaires.

A last word on company stock: If you've acquired any through your plan, your employer may give you the option of selling it back or taking it with you. If you feel it's worth holding on to, consider opening an IRA at a brokerage firm, which can handle it for you; otherwise, sell it back and roll the proceeds into an IRA.

An annuity. A retirement annuity is an investment through an insurance company but sold through a variety of sources, such as mutual fund companies, brokers, and banks. It begins paying you a fixed income when you retire (or at some other specified date) and can continue for the rest of your life if you choose that option. There are those who swear by annuities, thrilled they will always have an income, even if it does not include a cost-of-living adjustment. Be aware, though, that you could make an expensive mistake with an annuity (some, for example, charge a variety of fees); a little research to figure out the differences among annuities and/or some independent advice can help you find the one best suited to you.

Which should you choose? Many experts suggest that the IRA is preferable to an annuity. Since the money being rolled over is already tax-deferred, you could get the benefits of an annuity with none of the costs—which might run several percent of your assets per year—plus easier access for changing your investments. Your plan or an independent financial adviser can show you the pros and cons of the specific choices you have.

Go Directly to . . .

Remember, whatever kind of rollover account you decide on, the key word is *directly* (as in "Go directly to jail, do not pass GO . . ."). You could take a check from your employer and physically carry it to a mutual fund company or bank, but it would be foolish to do so. While there is no IRS penalty for handling it this way (if you do it within sixty days), it will introduce you to one of Uncle Sam's most aggravating Catch-22s.

While it was instituted to punish those who want to make real withdrawals from their accounts, it also catches the unknowledgeable and unwary. It can become your own little horror story, particularly if your account is substantial. Imagine the following scenario:

1. You're ready to take your money out of your old plan, but you don't make arrangements to transfer it into another tax-deferred account and simply ask for a check. The IRS requires your boss to withhold 20 percent of the balance. Why? It's security against your tax obligations to Uncle Sam, similar to the withholding taken from your paycheck.

2. You're left with your account balance less 20 percent. You decide to open your rollover, but since you're expected to roll over the entire amount, the IRS will want to know what happened to that 20 percent—as if they had nothing to do with it.

Now, if you can afford to replace the 20 percent into the rollover, you're okay—you can file for a refund of the withholding on your federal income tax.

3. But what if you can't come up with the 20 percent withheld by your old company? Imagine for a moment that you had a large account and that 20 percent withheld came to $15,000 —and you can't cover it when opening the new account. You now have to pay a 10 percent penalty for not rolling over the entire amount and you have to pay income tax on it as well.

This is outrageous, but there's nothing you can do about it. The moral of the story: Roll it over directly, or else. . . .

If you are doing a rollover to another 401(k), your new company will check out your old plan and give you instructions for asking your old company to make the transfer of funds (including the way the check should be issued). If you are rolling your funds into an IRA at a mutual fund or a bank, etc., they will take care of getting your money, once you have filled out the appropriate forms.

You Don't Have to Take It with You

There is one more alternative that may be open to you as you depart your company: You could leave your 401(k) where it is.

Yes, your company may actually let you leave your money in their plan after you've changed jobs, *if* you have more than $3,500 in your account. They might not encourage you to do it, though, because of the administrative costs to them.

Why would you want to leave your money with a former employer? If your 401(k) was a great deal, it could be your best option to let your money stay just where it is.

Some plans offer first-rate investment options that you'd have a tough time duplicating elsewhere. In addition, you sometimes get free access to funds that would charge you a commission if you were opening an IRA.

Fidelity, for example, charges no loads for most funds used for an IRA but none on *any* fund in a 401(k) if the plan sponsor has more than two hundred people. What does this mean to you? A deposit of $2,500 in Fidelity's well-known Magellan Fund starts working for you from the first dollar. If you were to roll over your 401(k) money into a Magellan IRA, you would start off by paying over 3 percent ($78), which means you begin with only $2,422. With a fund like AIM Constellation, with a 5.50 percent load, you'd lose over $138 putting that $2,500 in an IRA—but $0 by having it in a 401(k) that offers it.

In other words, by leaving your money where it is, you could start out a bit ahead—and every bit counts.

> While many 401(k)s absorb all administrative costs, if you switch to a mutual fund IRA and diversify into several funds, each may cost you $10 or more per year.

Of course, staying in your former employer's plan doesn't mean you get all its benefits. Obviously, since you no longer are an active employee, you cannot make any further deposits in your account. More important, benefits like the loan feature are no longer open to you. Weighing all the pros and cons, however, it can still be a good deal.

Retirement

Before going any further, here's one piece of advice I will give you without reservation:

> I know that many of you have never used a tax professional or financial planner before. But if you are thinking about retirement, you should consider consulting a specialist in 401(k) issues—particularly if you have a significant plan balance.

Retirement distributions are not only one of the most complex elements of your plan, but one of the most complex in the entire Internal Revenue Code. Your decisions will affect your cash flow and taxation in the years to come.

While your company may offer you advice in making retirement-related decisions, it could pay to have the advice of someone whose loyalty belongs to you alone.

"Can I Retire Now?"

When can you retire and have access to your 401(k) money?

- **If you want to pack it in early** and your plan allows this option, you can retire at any age and still have access to your 401(k). There is, however, a penalty for early distribution unless you take it in *at least* five equal, yearly payments based on life expectancy. They must last until you are *at least* 59½ and are taxed as you receive them. (Once you take these payments, you could take a lump-sum payment after 59½, but receive no special tax treatment.)

- **If you decide to extend your working career** (or have other sources of income), you can push off dipping into your 401(k) until the spring after you're 70½. At this point, you must begin distribution or face a 50 percent penalty of the required distribution. (More about this shortly.)

- **If you have reached age 59½,** you can draw on your plan account without penalty. You can take it in a single payment with special tax averaging, roll it over into an annuity or IRA, or get the payout chosen by your employer.

Your Options

Your first two options as a retiree—rolling it over to an IRA or annuity or taking a distribution—are slightly different from your options when leaving a job. You may also have a third choice: a payout.

Rollover. Actually, a rollover is a lump-sum distribution, but with limited "lumps" for you. As with the rollover previously described, you have to find an appropriate new investment for your money and watch over it, but there's no withdrawal penalty after 59½ and no immediate taxes.* However, once you roll your money out of the 401(k), you no longer qualify for special tax treatment that treats the distribution as if paid over a number of years. (See below.)

You must start taking a minimum distribution no later than April 1 after you reach age 70½—or pay a penalty of 50 percent of the amount that you should have taken—based on the overall balance of *all* your IRAs. The institutions holding your IRAs might be able to help sort this out.

Your account can also be rolled over into an annuity, which offers regular payments and a variety of death benefits, as well as higher management fees than an IRA. (See page 141.) This is an area where an outside professional can be extremely useful— as it can in choosing between an IRA and an annuity.

Lump-sum distribution. The "lumps" in this distribution are the possibility of paying too much in taxes. You can, however, reduce your obligations in two ways:

- If you were born before January 1, 1936, you can do ten-year averaging, using 1986 tax rates. Your balance is taxed as if paid over ten years. (Any contributions made before 1974 may be treated as capital gains and taxed in a lump sum according to current rates.)
- If you are over 59½, you can use five-year averaging. Your balance is taxed as if paid over five years.

In order to take advantage of these reductions, you must have been in the plan for five tax years before the year you first take a distribution.

---

*You could roll over only a portion of your account and take the rest in a lump sum, but you lose the option of averaging.

Is special tax treatment better than a rollover? It depends on your personal situation. You should consider advice offered by your plan or look to a financial adviser who knows 401(k)s for the information needed to make an informed choice.

Payout. What's the best way to take a payout from your plan? There are a number of ways that this can be done, with none the obvious choice for everyone. It will depend on a wide variety of factors, including your marital status, the ages and health of both you and your spouse/beneficiary, the return offered by an annuity versus what you think you can get on your own, etc.

Of course, your opinion may not matter at all. If you haven't chosen to take a lump-sum distribution, your plan's documents will spell out exactly how you will be paid.

Your plan may choose to cut you loose and buy you an annuity with your money. On the other hand, it may give you a choice of payment methods through the plan administrator: for example, based on your life expectancy, in equal installments that allow your account to keep growing, or the opportunity to draw on your money as needed.

Are you planning to put off drawing on your 401(k) for as long as possible? Then be on the lookout for an important reminder from your plan administrator as you approach age 70½: You must take your minimum distribution on the following April 1 or lose 50 percent of it as a penalty. Perhaps even more important, you also must choose how your withdrawals will be calculated.

Why should you care about this "accountant stuff"? *Because it will affect your cash flow and taxation.* Most experts seem to agree that you're better off with one method: You lock in a payout based on your life expectancy, or yours and your spouse's/

beneficiary's, computed with actuarial tables.* (For example, if this number is twenty-five years, you get ¹/₂₅th the first year, ¹/₂₄th the second, ¹/₂₃rd the third, and so on.) The plan continues to pay you, your beneficiary, or your estate under the original terms chosen until the account is depleted. This means lower current and estate taxes, and the opportunity for the account to keep growing. Even if you are single or do not care about your estate, this choice can affect your current finances.

However, if you don't state this preference (called "term-certain") to your plan's administrators, you could get a different choice by default—and it's irreversible.

This alternative starts out similarly, but changes dramatically when one party dies and payments are recalculated based on the survivor's life expectancy. The result: higher payments, *higher taxes,* and an account *depleted* much sooner. When both parties die, a lump sum is paid to his/her estate—and taxed immediately. (As you can see, I wasn't exaggerating when I said retirement distributions were complicated.)

> In the end, you have responsibility for seeing that your distributions are handled in the best way for you. That's why you should consider discussing this issue with a financial adviser who is 401(k)-savvy.

Merging your plans. A new alternative has just been born, offering an interesting option to those of you lucky enough to have both a pension and a 401(k). Benefits consultant William M. Mercer Inc. has shown clients how a 401(k) balance can be merged into a traditional pension. The result is a monthly payout similar to an annuity—but without the high fees involved—that offers professional money management on all your money. It's not well known at this point, but things could change.

---

*If your spouse is significantly younger than you, a loophole permits you to lower your payouts dramatically if that is to your benefit. For any other beneficiary—for example, a child—the difference in ages for computation purposes is no more than ten years.

A Parting "Reward" from Uncle Sam

If you have been diligent in building your account—starting early and maxing out your contributions—Uncle Sam has a special kind of "reward" for you: a *success* penalty for any year when you receive more than $150,000, which amounts to an extra 15 percent tax on the excess.

Using the five-year averaging technique mentioned earlier, this means that the maximum lump-sum distribution is $750,000 without having to pay additional tax ($750,000 divided by 5 is $150,000). So if you have $1 million in your account—not impossible if you start contributing $50 a week in your twenties—you'll pay an additional 15 percent tax on the last $50,000 each year ($1 million divided by 5 is $200,000; $200,000 less $150,000 is $50,000).

Outrageous? Yes—but just think of it as one small downside of being a millionaire!

What You Should Have Learned from This Chapter

1. When you leave your job, it may pay to leave your 401(k) where it is—if your plan was a superior one.
2. You can fall into a tax trap if you don't directly roll over your money from one tax-deferred account to another.
3. If your company allows it, you can take early retirement—and draw on your 401(k) before 59½ without penalty if you handle it correctly.
4. A financial adviser who knows about the specifics of 401(k)s can help you make the right decisions about distributions. Remember, in the end, you are responsible for seeing that your plan's distributions are handled appropriately.
5. There's a "success penalty"—obviously named by an IRS official with a sense of humor—for accumulating a jumbo-size 401(k).

10

Spending Your 401 (k) Prematurely: Use It and Lose It

This chapter deals with borrowing from your 401(k)—and why you shouldn't. It also suggests alternative methods of getting the money you need.

The 401(k) was invented for one reason, and one reason only: to help fund your retirement. And, as should be crystal clear by now, you're going to need it—all of it—in order to retire even reasonably well.

Unfortunately, not everyone sees it that way.

I saw one study of 401(k) participants that had a statistic I couldn't quite believe. It showed that 25 percent of participants wouldn't have joined a plan in the first place if there wasn't the promise of getting a loan on their accounts. Perhaps it's naïve to be surprised. After all, where else can most people accumulate a major amount of money—perhaps the biggest sum they ever had—that they can get their hands on?

> Unless you have a dire money emergency that cannot be solved any other way, tapping into your plan is one sure way of disappointing yourself down the road.

A Loan for All Reasons

What were the top reasons that people had for taking that loan? They wanted a new car. They needed a vacation. They had their eye on a new house.

It makes sense. After all, who doesn't want any of these? And, after all, you're not going to need the money in your account for a very long time. Right?

While any of these may sound like a good enough reason to use the money in your account, none of them is.

- A new car will be gone in a few years and what will you have left? *Nothing.*
- A vacation may "restart your engine," but where will you be in the long run? *Back where you started.*
- Even that dream house is not worth as much as your 401(k) account invested properly.

Once upon a time, as retirement approached, you could count on selling your house at a major profit and trading down to something that would leave you cash to live on. In today's real-estate environment, you can't count on getting a long-term return anywhere near the 10 percent per year that a stock fund might return to you.

Losing the Best of Your Plan

What happens when you take a loan from your 401(k)? It will vary somewhat from company to company (for example, some will not let you make new contributions to your plan until the loan has been repaid in full), but certain things always happen—and none of them are beneficial for your future.

Basically, you lose everything that's good about your plan.

- **You stop saving automatically.** All you're doing is trying to make up for lost time, not making your account grow. While you're actually making the loan to yourself—and paying yourself back—you're missing out on all the additional money that you should be accumulating. No tax-deferred deductions from your check, no compound interest.
- **You may miss out on one of those upswings in the stock market.** One little "bull" (upturn) can make a big difference in your long-term success.
- **If you decide to change jobs while the loan is outstanding, you can't pay it back later.** You're going to have to pay it back immediately. If you're unable to pay it back, then you'll have to take the amount as a distribution—and pay taxes and penalty on it. (Using it to buy a house may be an exception.)
- **You lose out on your company's matching contribution.** While you are paying off the amount of your loan, you're missing out on "free" money from matching—and there's no other way to get it.
- **You lose your safety net.** It's not there if you have the kind of emergency it was really made to cover in a pinch (see below).

My advice to you on this matter is short and sweet:

> Don't do it.

Borrowing or Spending It—and the Alternatives

Looking it over, however, taking a loan from your 401(k) is the least-worst of the mistakes you can make in the way you use it.

Situation #1: Taking a loan because "I've gotta have it."

Whether you want a vacation or an exercise machine, you don't even need an excuse to take a loan from your account—and 75 percent of plans allow them.

What happens: Usually, plans allow you to borrow up to 50 percent of the vested amount in your account (maximum: $50,000); some plans may let you borrow up to $10,000 even if this exceeds half your balance. (See your plan for details.) Very likely, there's a fee to set up the loan. You have to repay it on a regular basis within five years, charging yourself a rate that's 1 or 2 percent above the current prime—your company gets to set the exact amount. If the loan is for buying your primary residence, there's no regulatory limit on how long you can take to repay it, but it's usually no more than fifteen years.

Undoubtedly, the cost of the loan will be lower than you'd get at a bank, but you'll be missing out on the higher rates your investment options could be bringing.

If you leave your job before repaying the entire loan, the outstanding balance will be deducted from your account—which means you'll have to pay taxes and a penalty on it as a distribution. (See your plan's rules for housing-related loans.)

Your alternatives: For a car, see what kinds of bank loans are available and compare them with the promotional deals offered by the car manufacturers. For a vacation or any other relatively small purchase, you probably should be using a credit card. Every month, *Money* and *Kiplinger's* list the credit card providers that have the best rates for (a) people who pay their bills in total every month, and (b) people who run outstanding balances. You could cut your interest expenses in half if you're still paying the 18 to 19 percent that many are charging today.

You will lose some ground in building your account while your loan is outstanding, but you will eventually repay the original amount of your loan plus the interest set by your plan. It could be worse: You could have spent it.

Situation #2: You change your job.

You are leaving your job and want to have just-in-case money.

What happens: You'll have 20 percent withheld by your employer for the IRS if you take possession of your money, even momentarily. If you deposit it into your checking account, you'll have to pay taxes and a penalty if you haven't reached retirement. (See Chapter 9.)

Your alternative: Back in 1988, I rolled over my first 401(k) into an IRA by sheer dumb luck—I guessed that it was the right thing to do. Today, it's more likely that your plan's administrator will give you material on keeping your money's tax-deferred status through a rollover, although you may not be exactly "encouraged" to keep it in your old plan. Any mutual fund company or bank will also have brochures available on the benefits of rolling over your money (and, of course, why they should be your choice of where to roll it over to).

Situation #3: You make a hardship withdrawal.

Under certain circumstances, specified by the IRS, some—but not all—plans permit you make a hardship withdrawal from your account. But make no mistake: You must prove true hardship, that is, have no other savings or source of money to:

- buy a house
- pay for your own/your children's/spouse's tuition
- avoid eviction
- pay major medical expenses.

What happens: Even if your withdrawal comes under this heading, you still have penalties and taxes to pay—and may not get back into your plan so easily if your finances turn around.

Your alternatives: Do you have salable assets? Will insurance cover your costs? Can you borrow from a commercial or other source at reasonable rates? You will have to answer no to all of these—as well as answer why taking a loan from your account will not satisfy your needs.

(You don't have to answer these questions directly to the Internal Revenue Service, but to your plan's administrator. In a way, this could be worse. Keeping your company's plan in compliance with IRS guidelines—so it doesn't get penalized—is his or her major concern.)

Eviction, major medical expenses, and the purchase of a home are the least likely to offer you easy alternatives. You are more likely to be able to handle college expenses in another way.

Have you tried the possibilities of loans from the college itself, from the federal government's Stafford and PLUS programs, or from various foundation and private sources? You should try any or all of these before going through the hassle of trying to make a hardship withdrawal from a 401(k). (Access to a credit union loan or a home equity loan needs to be exhausted as well, with the latter at least making the interest tax deductible.)

Money, Kiplinger's, and *Smart Money* all offer frequent rundowns on how to pay for college. Ask your local branch librarian about back issues of these magazines or on-line assistance and for help in finding what you want. If you need further help in finding out your alternatives, ask for some assistance in browsing through the appropriate section of your local bookstore.

Note: There are a few other circumstances under which you are entitled to a plan distribution:

- death, in which case the account is passed, tax free, to your spouse (but taxable to any other beneficiary)

- disability, when it's taxable but without penalty
- divorce, if possession is given to your ex-spouse
- termination of your company's plan or the sale of your company, when it may be rolled over

Your plan can give you specifics relative to its rules and a financial adviser can help minimize your tax liabilities.

One More Time . . .

Spending your 401(k) prematurely doesn't make sense. Yet it is a risk taken by people who wouldn't think of crossing the street against a red light. Depleting or purposely setting back your goals is one sure way to lose track of that *vision* I spoke about earlier: a solid retirement.

What You Should Have Learned
from This Chapter

1. If you borrow from your plan, you may pay a lower interest rate than you'd get at a bank, but you lose all the advantages of being in the plan—including matching contributions.
2. Long-term appreciation on a house you buy today is unlikely to match the 10 percent long-term return that stocks have shown.
3. Loans for "lifestyle" reasons should probably be done, instead, with your credit card or other sources. *Money* or *Kiplinger's* might suggest where to find a better interest rate than you're currently paying.
4. If you change jobs while a loan is outstanding, you'll pay a distribution penalty for the unpaid balance.
5. Hardship withdrawals are hard to justify—unless you can prove you have absolutely no place else to turn.

PART V

Putting It Together

Off and Running
(*plus* Your "To Do" List)

Remember that chapter called "Yes, You *Can* Be an Investor!"? Well, guess what? You've already started the process by reading this book.

But don't stop now—you can't afford to.

> You've got to keep acting and thinking like an investor for the next decade or three—until you are ready to put your feet up and relax. (Even then, you'll still have to keep your eyes on the investments in your account.)

By that time, your money, ideally, will have grown significantly through the powers of compound interest, asset allocation, and at least some investing in stock funds. Statistics show that you should not only be better off than you would have been in what you once thought of as a "low risk" way to "save," but you'll have the satisfaction of having played an important role in shaping your own future.

In the meantime, here are some final suggestions for making sure you make the most of your plan—a "to do" list to keep your 401(k) working hard to get you where you want to go.

1. Keep contributing.

In the course of the book, I showed you how *time* can be your best friend in investing—that starting early can make a big difference in your final account balance, even if you stop after just ten years (see page 29). But if you don't stop, the combination of time and *regular deposits* can be extremely potent allies in growing your account as large as you can.

2. Contribute as much as you can.

A third element that can help you grow your account to its maximum size is the *amount of your contribution.* If contributing $25 a week can get you to half a million dollars (more with company matching), think what $50 or $100 can do. As your salary increases, remember to increase the percent that goes into your plan. Keeping up with the Joneses is not as important as keeping ahead of inflation.

3. Shift your asset allocation as your age increases.

While an 80 percent investment in aggressive growth stock funds is great when you're twenty-five, you should reconsider your asset allocation as you hit the landmarks of your life and adjust it accordingly. This doesn't necessarily mean heading for the rocking chair: You'd be surprised how many people who considered themselves just "average" investors when they were younger become much more aggressive as they reach fifty or older.

4. Be as aggressive an investor as you reasonably can.

As I've said, the experts agree that you can better afford higher risks when you're twenty-five than when you're sixty. But this doesn't mean to accept an aggressive growth or emerging markets fund just because it's riskier. Read up on its performance and get any other information you can before deciding whether to make your allocation to it.

5. Keep track of how you're doing.

No one but you has the responsibility for running your account—and making sure your investments are working for you. Know when to switch funds because of poor fund performance or to rebalance your account because you've done better in one sector and it has skewed your allocation—for example, from 60 percent in stocks to 70 percent—unless that's the way you want it.

6. Ask your plan for changes if you think you need them.

If you are truly unhappy about the performance of the investment options being offered by your plan, then speak up about it—and have good reasons for thinking that other types or specific funds should be part of the plan. Let your benefits office know your concerns; they can't know what's on your mind if you don't tell them.

7. Encourage your fellow workers to participate —and help them.

Remember when you used to be unsure about your prowess as an investor? There are others in your company who probably still think that way. Let them know what they are missing by not being part of the plan—and the benefits (including any matching funds from the company) that are available only to those who participate.

8. Talk over your options with people you trust.

You don't know anyone who plays the stock market? Don't bet on it—the most unlikely candidates (from your point of view, at least) may have started their own investment club or are dare-devils on their own. So talk to your friends, your coworkers, even your mother-in-law. . . . You never know who might be able to help.

9. Keep reading/watching/going on-line to learn as much as you can.

We all think we have too much information in our lives (and it's probably true), but some of it is definitely worth having. When it comes to being an investor, up-to-date information is vital. The laws change, the rules change, the economic climate changes—and they all affect your 401(k). Information is your best weapon in wringing every nickel you can out of your account. All those publications and television shows mentioned back in Chapter 5 can help you—and there are always new ones to be on the lookout for.

10. Keep believing you can do better—if you try.

Don't be discouraged if your funds go up and down along the way. Nobody promised you that investing was going to be easy—or easy on your nerves. Short-term setbacks are one aspect of long-term investing that no one can do anything about—unless you want to sit on the sidelines and put your money in a savings account paying 3 percent. Taking risks is hard, but there's the promise of getting something for doing it: a better return and a better future.

Appendix

Toll-Free Numbers for
Major Mutual Fund Families

As mentioned throughout the text, the major mutual fund companies offer a wealth of free or low-cost information to investors, whether or not you currently own any of their funds.

IDS*	800-328-8300
Dreyfus	800-373-9387
Fidelity	800-544-8888
Janus	800-525-8983
Merrill Lynch	800-637-3863
Oppenheimer	800-525-7048
T. Rowe Price	800-541-8832
Putnam	800-225-1581
Charles Schwab	800-890-9293
Scudder	800-225-2470
Twentieth Century	800-345-2021
Vanguard	800-420-2676

*Funds of American Express Financial Services.

Index